Learning On The Fly And Laughing Till I Cry

A Journal of Mothering My Daughter From Ages One to Seven

Deb Preston

BRIGHTER SIDE
PUBLISHING

Learning on the Fly and Laughing Till I Cry:
A Journal of Mothering My Daughter From Ages One to Seven

Published by Brighter Side Publishing

Edited by Maria Noble

Cover design by James Henry Dufresne

Cover art by Ari Preston

For information about special discounts for bulk purchases, please contact Brighter Side Publishing at hello@brightersidepublishing.com.

ISBN 979-8-9873434-1-8 (hardcover)
ISBN 979-8-9873434-0-1 (paperback)

Printed in the United States of America

This book is dedicated to my daughter, Ari,
who has bestowed upon me the great joy and honor of
holding the title of Mom.

And to Nedra. Oh, how I wish we had more time with you
but I can still hear your laughter, even from heaven, and know
you are here with us.

Table of Contents

Introduction

This is not a book in the usual sense of the term. It's more of a journal...a collection of my thoughts and experiences, highs and lows, and most defining moments so far, not just as a parent, but as a human.

See, when I became a mother for the first time, I felt very isolated and alone in my experiences. So on my daughter's first birthday, I decided to start sharing those experiences with others. I figured there were probably other parents in the same boat and maybe if we could laugh and cry and share and reflect and relate to and with one another...maybe we wouldn't feel so alone anymore. So I started to write.

These pages contain my thoughts from the time my daughter turned one year old until she turned seven. They follow and record my transformation from unrealistic perfectionist to hopeless hot mess to an even-keeled mother who can much more easily recognize what's important and what's not.

Some days, my daughter would say or do something that would make me rethink my entire approach to life. Other days, I simply wanted to share her crazy antics, to throw my hands up in the air and say to someone else who would understand, "What in the world..."

Some days, I had pages worth of reflection pouring out of my heart and mind and other days, just a sentence or two. But every day, I wanted to approach life and more specifically, motherhood, with transparency, an open mind, simple wonder, and humor.

My hope is that as you read these pages, you can relate on a soul level. I hope that you can appreciate and reflect on the lessons parenthood teaches us about life and love and ourselves. I hope you can feel encouraged knowing you're not the only one who has failed their children or themselves...but believe with all of your heart that you're never too far gone to learn, adjust your approach, and try again. And I hope you can laugh until you cry at my most head-scratching, face-palming moments.

None of us are perfect. We never will be. But together...we're stronger.

CHAPTER 1 | FAILING

YEAR 1 | DAY 1

I'll always distinctly remember the first time I saw her little face. I didn't know how to be a mother. When the doctor held her up to me so that I could be the first to kiss her, I didn't even know where to kiss her, it felt so foreign and overwhelming.

For the first few months of her life, I struggled to learn selflessness. I cried from exhaustion and wondered if I was doing things right.

And then we grew. She began to grow bigger and stronger and more independent and I began to grow into the person I was always meant to be, more loving, more selfless, more confident.

I came to know every little thing about her, big and small, and fell in love with every detail. I love the way she laughs when she knows she did something funny. She doesn't just laugh to herself but she leans in and connects with my eyes and the deepest part of me and we laugh together.

I love the way she and I sleep in identical positions and make the same scrunchy face, that she just has that part of me inside of her. I love her sense of rhythm that Daddy gave her and the widow's peak he gave her too, even though it means her wild hair is always in her eyes.

I love walking into her room every morning to pick her up from her crib and to find out if she's playing peekaboo with her blanket that morning, or offering me a chew on her blanket tag, or diving onto her stomach to pretend

4

she's still sleeping. I love her two whole teeth and her crystal blue eyes and how she pulls out the dog's loose hairs and tries to feed them to him.

When she acts up and fights to stubbornly assert her own will and I'm searching for the patience to wait her out, I think about how much I love her strong, independent spirit and how I'll teach her to channel and use it, and how she'll make a difference in the world one day because she's so determined.

I thank God every day for her and every day I pray that He would help me to raise her well. In good times and bad, she's the very best part of me.

Now to hope she doesn't figure out walking…

YEAR 1 | DAY 39

Today, my child bruised her nose falling into a bath faucet, tried to eat a bandaid off of her finger and cried when I fished it out of her mouth, and made me believe she might have eaten the rubber piece off a spring doorstop (she didn't). Yay, toddlers!

YEAR 1 | DAY 115

I handed my daughter her shorts while I was changing her diaper today and said, "Hold these, they stink!" She held them up to her nose, took a deep, dramatic whiff, and whispered, "ahhhhh!" like they smelled amazing. She is her father's child.

One of the greatest joys in life is climbing into bed knowing that your husband is waking up with your toddler the next morning.

YEAR 1 | DAY 221

Have you ever had one of those days where your kid spits up on you...twice...and you think you cleaned it okay but the dog keeps trying to lick your legs? Then you pick up Subway® for dinner because you're too exhausted to cook and you drop your sandwich and it lands wide open, face down on your shag area rug? Then you put your kid to bed and have wine and cookie dough for dinner?

No? Oh. Me neither.

YEAR 1 | DAY 229

Me (whispering into my daughter's ear): Shhhh...you're my favorite person! Am I your favorite person?

Daughter (whispering into my ear): Shhhh...Dada!

FAILING

YEAR 1 | DAY 276

People/things I've yelled at this morning for nearly waking my daughter ten minutes too early:

1. My dog for walking with a jangly collar
2. An Elmo doll for making a noise when I stepped on him
3. My husband for using the NutriBullet – "Why do you need a shake?! Eat cereal quietly."

YEAR 1 | DAY 364

Some days, my kid tells me when she needs to use the potty, we attend story time and a gym class, visit with family, and learn 251 new things. Other days (like the very next day), I'm crawling around the carpet trying to find the starting point of a pee trail I just stepped in and letting her watch the same movie 175 times in a row. At this moment, she's holding and using my hand as a fork to pick up mandarin slices and put them in her mouth because I've just accepted defeat.

YEAR 2 | DAY 54

Today I told my child, "Choose one stuffy to take in the car." She chose Elmo, two giraffes, a rubber duck, a half-eaten waffle, and a plastic potato.

I can't actually *see* her in her carseat, but the pile of toys is moving. Close enough.

YEAR 2 | DAY 71

I am a perfectionist. Or at least, I was.

By twenty, I had completed my bachelor's degree with honors and launched a professional career. While acquiring my master's, I set a goal not to miss a single point on any assignment or test, and achieved it in several classes.

I drove myself to be the top performer in every position I held and was frequently promoted. My success and the approval I received from professors and employers made up a substantial part of my identity. And then I left my challenging, rewarding, influential position with a prestigious tech company to stay home with my new baby.

When I originally decided to stay at home, I thought it only fair that I do all of the meal planning, shopping, cooking, cleaning, money management, and household errands. I imagined a structured schedule that included reading, singing, tummy time, and regular story times at the library.

I sincerely didn't understand why some stay-at-home parents couldn't manage to do all of those things. They had eight to ten *hours* every day to knock it out. I mean… what were they doing with their time?!

Then she arrived, eating every two to three hours, spitting up every time she ate, peeing every two to three minutes, crying for no apparent reason, and never letting me sleep for longer than two hours at a time for the first three months of her life. We immediately scrapped our

14

Saturday morning cleaning routine. We ate fast food for most meals because we were too exhausted to cook, let alone grocery shop. I begrudgingly abandoned the idea of a structured schedule as we shifted into survival mode.

My husband and I constantly held fatigue battles. *You're nauseous with a headache? Well, my migraine has struck me pretty much blind. Yeah. It's super serious.*

Some days, my daughter and I managed to attend story time, grocery shop, and even brush her two teeth. I felt like I was finally "getting it." But "failure" days immediately followed, where I didn't leave the house, didn't shower, didn't change her out of pajamas, and watched more TV than I intended just to keep her in one place and give myself a much-needed break.

I didn't always accomplish what I had set out to do in a given day, sometimes not even in a few days. And although I managed our finances, I felt like a lesser person for not contributing to them.

I had hit an all-time low. It felt as if I had no value or use to the world outside of "babysitting." I felt like a failure.

Then a few months ago, my husband was out and it was just my daughter and I in her room. I had closed the door to trap her inside and was mindlessly flipping through my phone as she played on the floor. It was another lazy parenting night.

I was playing old songs from my phone when I noticed she start waving her arms to the music. As she stood on the floor, I shook her arms and hips to make her dance like a little puppet. She laughed so hard she was gasping for air.

I picked her up and started bouncing, twirling, dipping, and throwing her to the beat. I hadn't laughed so hard and so genuinely in maybe ten years.

For as simple of a moment as it was, it was the best moment of my whole life. It suddenly struck me that my daughter didn't know or care about our schedule, that we weren't getting social interaction, or that our house wasn't spotless.

She was just happy to be with me and to spend time with me. She loved me – even though I had failed miserably at perfection. I realized the only thing that *truly* mattered in my role as a stay-at-home parent was loving her.

My only "failure" was not allowing for and adjusting to imperfection. I was insisting on perfection despite the fact that I didn't have the time, energy, or resources to achieve it. I wasn't recognizing the utter importance of my own mental, emotional, and physical health and capabilities, and not taking them into consideration before adding another task to my list.

My failure was attempting to make everything an equal and top priority, rather than determining what was *most* important. Was it more important to me to make the bed or to use those five minutes to snuggle with my child while she still fit in my lap?

I still strive to take my daughter to story times, play gyms, parks, and other activities important to her development. But I've learned to accept and enjoy lazy days at home, too. I've found that taking more time for myself, even if it means dinner dishes wait until the morning, has made me a better mother and person.

This imperfect perfectionist has learned to say no to guilt and busy-ness, and yes to grace and a more meaningful life. It turns out imperfection is inevitable so instead of fighting it, I'm choosing to be realistic about my capabilities and prioritize what's most important to me.

Prioritizing and adjusting accordingly doesn't make you a failure after all. It makes you a success.

YEAR 2 | DAY 103

I don't like being a stay-at-home mom. There. I said it.

So many moms gush about how much they love staying at home with their kids, how their passion has always been children, how they've dreamed of being a stay-at-home mom since they were a little girl. I envy those women. And I feel awful because of them, because I am not on the same page.

Reading children's books, watching children's shows and movies, learning and practicing things like colors and numbers…it's mind-numbing at times. Yes, it's extremely rewarding to see my child learn and grow. I can't tell you how many teeny tiny things I've proudly announced to my husband that our daughter has learned or said while he was at work. But the process of getting there is monotonous.

When I first decided to stay home with our daughter until she started school, I imagined being almost like a preschool teacher to her. I would look up crafts and projects for us to work on that were developmentally appropriate. I would teach her letters and numbers using flashcards with pictures of apples and xylophones on them. But once I got started, I realized that I didn't actually like or enjoy any of those things.

I take my daughter to story times at the library, classes and play times at Gymboree, and any free or cheap local activities – free movies over the summer, carnivals, petting zoos, you name it! But I never feel very excited to go. In fact, I distinctly do *not* like going to story time. But I know it's great for my daughter's development and that she loves getting out with other kids and trying new and different things, so I take her to everything I can find.

I like drawing with my daughter and helping her to act out movies with stuffed animals...for about 30 minutes. Then I kiss and hug her and encourage her to keep playing while I pick up around the house or do a little writing. I'm not the type of mom who likes or wants to play one-on-one all day long.

Honestly, I believe that playing by herself has helped her to develop an amazing imagination. Or maybe that's just what I tell myself to feel better about it.

Staying at home has also slowly killed my social skills. I used to be able to strike up a conversation with anyone, anywhere. Now I flounder in social settings and spend the next hour after I've left replaying the conversations and wincing at things I said that I assume sounded stupid or insensitive. I second-guess and overanalyze how I must have come across to people.

I don't work out as often and don't wear anything trendy or cute or flirty most days. Comfort is the name of the game when your plans for the day include having your hair brushed by your toddler using a plastic toy fork.

And yet...my daughter will only be this age once. And that knowledge causes me to cherish every single moment of every action-packed, exciting day as well as every monotonous day spent with her. I miss these days before they're even gone yet, with the full understanding of just how precious this time with her is.

The fact is that even though I miss the challenge of working at a more traditional job, solving complex issues and actually meeting with real live people, I do not *want* to work full-time unless and until she's in school full-time. I don't want to work eight hours a day and commute another hour, only to enjoy a few rushed hours with her before her 7:30 bedtime.

I would be jealous of anyone else who got to spend these boring days with her. It would feel as if they were somehow stealing the time I want, stealing the role I want...but don't want.

The truth is that staying home with her is the best thing for our entire family right now. I get to be a part of nearly every moment of her few precious years at home. I have the privilege of helping to shape her character and her mind.

Because we're able to stay in our own home, my husband, who works from home, can visit with his daughter during breaks and lunches. He can occasionally enjoy a tiny visitor bursting through his office door to yell, "I'm a duck!", quack in his face, and run away giggling.

And because I can take care of most of the housework while I'm home and watching our daughter, my husband and I don't have the stress of trying to knock out housework and errands *and* spend quality time with our daughter within a few evening hours. We're enjoying more balance and peace in our lives.

I don't like being a stay-at-home mom. It's not my dream and not even really my "thing." And that's totally okay.

I don't have to love watching cartoons, learning colors, singing the Hokey Pokey for the 276th time at story time, playing pretend all day, or rarely finding an occasion to dress nicely. We all have different personalities and preferences. Not loving staying at home doesn't mean that I don't love my daughter.

I don't like being a stay-at-home mom. But I'm cherishing every moment with her and creating a more balanced and peaceful atmosphere in our home. I'm 110% available every time that little voice calls, "Mommy!" And that's all that really matters.

YEAR 2 | DAY 118

I have officially given up on the day. My daughter spilled an entire bowl of bran cereal (made of the tiniest pellets known to man) on our shag area rug because she was trying to feed it to Elmo. She was very upset he had cereal stuck in his fur and ran off with him while I vacuumed up.

I turned off the vacuum and heard running water. Sounds promising, no? I walked into the bathroom to find her standing at the sink on her little stairs, water running over Elmo's head, saying, "It's okay, Elmo. I help you!"

After wringing a good two cups of water out of Elmo, he's recovering in the laundry room. Jesus, take the wheeeeeel!

YEAR 2 | DAY 133

Thought I would hide in the pantry to sneak a brownie bite while my toddler wasn't looking. I congratulated myself on my *Bourne*-like stealth, only to get a huge hug from her a few minutes later. She pulled back, smelled my mouth, and said, "Hey, I smell chocolate!"

If you eat one more plant, you're coming inside! Do you understand?!

- things I say now

YEAR 2 | DAY 182

Currently deciding between:

1. Working out
2. Eating an entire pint of Ben & Jerry's

Please stop brushing my hair with your toes.

- things I say now

YEAR 2 | DAY 199

No matter what I dress her in, my daughter has added a superhero cape, firefighter hat, and movie star sunglasses to the ensemble...for three days now...to parks, story times, grocery stores, and church. Prayers appreciated.

YEAR 2 | DAY 207

As my daughter gets older, she's doing a lot more things that remind me of myself or my husband. That's my scrunched up face she's making. That's my husband's ~~weirdness~~ creativity shining through.

This morning I was looking at her crib and sighing as I counted the stuffed animals she sleeps with every night. Twenty! Why does she even *have* twenty animals?! And why do they *all* have to squish into her bed with her?

My husband and I have tried to sneak away one or two at a time, animals we think she won't notice. But as we lower her into bed every night, she takes a quick inventory and calls out exactly who's missing. And she *cannot* rest until *all* of them are in her bed.

She loves every one of them with a fierce passion. If one goes missing, she won't rest until they're found. I can't distract her with another animal, a favorite movie, a snack, *anything* until they're back in her care.

Her huge giraffe, her tiny mouse, her "She-She" sheep that's been there since birth, her ladybug that her Gigi gave her just a few weeks ago...they're all equally important and irreplaceable in her heart.

And as I counted her animals this morning and sighed, I heard God's whisper in my ear, "She got that from Me." And I realized how fiercely God loves each of us. He knows us by name, remembers the tiniest details about us, and does not rest until we are safe in His care. Even when we feel like we don't matter, we are immeasurably important and irreplaceable to our Father.

Now when I see her animals, I don't see a toddler's annoying, selective attention to detail. I see a sweet reminder of God's love and fierce passion for each of us. And I treasure the way He hides His character in our children.

CHAPTER 2 | LISTENING

YEAR 2 | DAY 216

Dear new Elmo,

I don't mean to scare you, but you've got a hard life ahead of you. Your predecessors have died slow and painful deaths...which has led us to you.

You will be dragged around our home, our yard, our cars, and nearly every single destination to which we venture. Sometimes you'll make the journey safe in our daughter's warm embrace and sometimes held carelessly by your plastic eyeballs.

Your bright and fluffy fur will quickly dull and mat as you accumulate a film over your entire body, composed mostly of blueberry yogurt, dog slobber, and the germs found on the floors of a hundred different public places. Yuck. I know.

I won't be able to clean it for you, thanks to the battery box in your head and the sensors in your hands and belly. "Spot clean?" Right.

Your talking function won't last long, since my daughter will (a) overuse it and (b) drop you on your battery box a million times. Your mouth will become permanently stuck open. The velcro used to cover the battery box will stop sticking, leaving you with a gap in the back of your head. My daughter will then use that gap to drag you to the mailbox with us.

But...

You will experience a love that you likely wouldn't with most children. Because you will be my daughter's absolute best friend.

She'll talk to you from the moment she wakes up to the moment she falls asleep at night, offering you everything she has. She'll ask if you want to share grapes with her, if you're thirsty, if you want to color, what color crayon you prefer, and if you're scared of the dinosaur in her movie (and then reassure you, "It's okay. I got you!").

She'll teach you to share, take turns, be kind, pee in the potty, eat vegetables, and every other lesson that I'm trying to teach her. She'll even teach you how to play the guitar, strumming the strings with your furry hands and enthusiastically cheering for every song you play.

She'll help you wash your hands and brush your teeth in her play kitchen sink. She'll tuck you in for naps, covering you in a blanket, singing you Twinkle Twinkle, and telling you not to be afraid and that she loves you. She's loved you since she was eight months old and now, at almost three years, she loves you even more.

And when you've reached your absolute limit, when your fur is just a matted film, you can no longer talk, and you've reached an almost embarrassing level of stench, I'll take good care of you, Elmo. I'll wrap you up nicely and add you to the others hidden away in my closet. You've received so much love and played an integral part in so many memories that I can't bear not to keep you. And one day when my daughter is grown, I'll take you out of hiding to share with her all over again.

It's a hard life you're embarking on, but it's the sweetest one you'll find. Good luck, Elmo!

YEAR 2 | DAY 224

Today my daughter acted out a dramatic fall down a playground slide, then played dead at the bottom for a full minute, despite my attempts to "wake her up." The other parents were not impressed.

YEAR 2 | DAY 238

Oh, crib. I remember when I felt an unusual surge of energy at eight months pregnant and decided to surprise my husband by assembling you while he was at work. And after completing your assembly in the living room, tightening every screw and placing the sheets with extra care, realizing that you didn't fit through the nursery door.

Oh, crib. I remember my husband *dis*assembling you in the living room and *re*assembling you in the nursery after a long day at work.

Oh, crib. I remember placing my sleeping newborn in your care, sneaking out of her room like a ninja, and telling my dog things like, "Stop jangling your collar!" You kept her safe each night while my husband and I ate takeout and caught up on our favorite TV shows.

And although it's exciting to be moving our daughter into a big girl bed this weekend, I feel much sadder than I had anticipated. Because disassembling you means packing away a phase of our lives.

And yes, that phase was challenging and exhausting but there was such a sweetness to it all. My daughter will never reach her arms up to me to be lifted out of her bed again.

She'll also never be trapped in one place for two hours of nap time, so that I can enjoy me time. That's a real bummer.

Oh, crib. I'd love to store you away with her baby clothes and toys but alas, you're much too big. So instead, we'll give you to another family, and to another set of parents in desperate need of takeout and their favorite TV shows.

YEAR 2 | DAY 243

I'm drinking a caramel frappé.

Daughter: I want some!

Me: No, baby. This is coffee.

Daughter: That's not coffee. That's ice cream!

Smart girl.

YEAR 2 | DAY 280

Me: Do you know you're my favorite girl in the whole world?! If they lined up all the girls in the world and I could choose *any* of them, I would choose you!

Daughter: Awww! I would choose Tía! (her aunt)

Toddlers are so sweet.

YEAR 2 | DAY 281

Today's lesson: No matter how nice it feels when she plays with your hair, do *not* let your toddler "give you a ponytail." It will not end well.

YEAR 2 | DAY 303

Rookie me: Do you want celery and carrots?

Toddler: No.

Wiser, older me: Do you want yummy vegetables from Daniel Tiger's garden?

Toddler: Yeeeees! Broccoli, too?!

Sucker.

YEAR 2 | DAY 324

This morning, I hit the ground running. I woke up before my family to start cleaning the house and checking things off my to-do list.

Me and my two shots of espresso were on a roooooolllllllllll...until my two-year-old daughter climbed up on the couch and called to me while I was wiping down the kitchen counters, "Momma, you wanna cuddle me?"

As I opened my mouth to tell her that no, momma had to finish cleaning first, I tried to remember the last time she slowed down from playing like a maniac and actually requested a cuddle. And I couldn't remember.

So I set down my sponge, washed my hands, and snuggled up next to my daughter to watch *Curious George* together, she with her chocolate milk, me with my coffee.

Yes, it slowed down my progress. Yes, it's made for a much busier afternoon. But I wouldn't have traded that moment, or that chocolate milk, or that curious monkey that ruins everything and actually breaks a lot of laws with zero repercussions, for anything.

Because when my daughter is older and has left the house, she won't remember clean countertops or freshly mopped floors. She'll remember cuddling on the couch with her momma. And those are the kind of memories I'm interested in creating.

New nutrition standards: No, you can't eat a chocolate bunny until you finish your chicken nuggets.

YEAR 2 | DAY 348

What does the Man in the Yellow Hat do for a living? He has an apartment in the city, a house in the country, and is friends with museum curators, train conductors, and astronauts. *Also*, with George's history of wrecking *all. the. things*, why does anyone think it's a good idea to send him into outer space?

LISTENING

YEAR 2 | DAY 349

Me: What's your donkey doing with that salt and pepper?

Two-year-old: That's not salt and pepper! (looks at me like I've lost my mind) Those are binoculars...he's a jungle donkey!! (sighs to herself)

Obviously.

YEAR 2 | DAY 361

I hate coloring. I might even use the word *despise*.

And yet, here I am, sitting with my almost-three-year-old, sighing to myself as I attempt to color tiny details with a fat-tipped Crayola marker. Why?

Because I recently read a quote by Catherine M. Wallace, "Listen earnestly to anything [your children] want to tell you, no matter what. If you don't listen eagerly to the little stuff when they are little, they won't tell you the big stuff when they are big, because to them all of it has always been big stuff."

I know that coloring is one of my daughter's favorite activities. I'm choosing to take part in something that she loves, something that feels like "the big stuff" to her at three years old.

Because one day, she'll be facing truly big stuff. Raising her will become more complicated than remembering what she named her stuffed animals (the names change every day – hooray!). I won't always be able to cheer her up by simply making our dog "say" funny things. And it will take much more than a bandaid and sticker to heal her broken heart.

And when that day comes, I want her to know and trust beyond a shadow of a doubt that if she invites me into her "big stuff," I won't hesitate for even one second to jump in and join her. Because I've always joined her in her "big stuff."

46

LISTENING

Today I'm being mindful not to overlook the little stuff. Because "...to them all of it has always been big stuff."

YEAR 2 | DAY 364

Today our ferocious, 10-year-old, 24-pound, Jack Russell dog...ate Jesus. Let me explain. We're attempting to teach our toddler that Jesus lives in her heart.

Toddler (eating pancakes): Here Jesus, here's canpakes. (Informs me) He's in my heart. (Pretends to reach into her chest, then holds her hand out to show me) Look, here he is! (Gasps dramatically) Oh, no! I dropped him! (Jumps out of her chair to look around the floor) Jesus! Where *are* you?! (Yells at our dog) Nooooo! (Upset, tells me) Bubba ate Jesus!!

Me: He didn't eat Jesus! *Please* pick Jesus up and put him back in your heart!

I think my work here is done!

LISTENING

YEAR 3 | DAY 21

I'm sitting here listening to my three-year-old argue with a stuffed hippo in her bed about whether they should leave the room.

Hippo: We awake!

Three-year-old: But mommy said wait for heeeeer!

I wonder who will win.

Front-facing car seats make it so much harder to secretly eat things that I don't want to share with my child. I miss the good old days...

YEAR 3 | DAY 28

My daughter's summary of her class at church: Joseph was sleeping. And you know that wee little man? It's Jesus in my heart. Jesus and a hippo.

Seems legit.

YEAR 3 | DAY 30

In case you were wondering how toddler parenting is going in our house, I just fed my kid meatballs and blueberries for dinner and felt *super* triumphant about it. So...there's that.

If you like listening to "Shake It Off" 167 times in a row, you might like being a parent!

YEAR 3 | DAY 43

Me at 12:05 (settling into recliner): I'm gonna take a little break from coloring with you.

Three-year-old at 12:06: Phew! That was a good break. Back to work!

YEAR 3 | DAY 54

Names I've had to call my daughter in the last month because she was so deep in character she wouldn't respond to her actual name:

1. Silver (a superhero)
2. Marker (a kid who solves problems)
3. Steve (a character from *Curious George*)
4. Catzilla (a ferocious cat who only speaks in growls and even prayed over dinner tonight in growls)

Parenting: Keeping me guessing since 2015.

YEAR 3 | DAY 70

Me: (making my child's bed amidst 105 stuffed animals, sweating profusely)

Husband: (laying on the couch doing literally nothing)

Child: Mooooom, I need your help fixing this toy!

My favorite part of being a parent is trying to pee while my 3-year-old knocks on the door yelling, "Trick or treat!"

YEAR 3 | DAY 101

I just cleaned my car – washed, vacuumed, wiped down. I basked in the temporary absence of stickers, goldfish crumbs, and small, dusty footprints on the back of my seat. And less than a week later, a plastic tub of popcorn emptied its buttery contents into the passenger seat as we turned out of the zoo parking lot.

Ever since I became a parent, *nothing* has stayed clean for longer than a few minutes. Not my car, not my house, not myself. But despite my hopeless longing for cleanliness and organization, being my three-year-old's momma is worth the mess.

Because if we hadn't gone to the zoo today, I would have missed her smiling from ear-to-ear on our way to the elephants, loudly announcing, "I love animals sooooo much!" I would have missed her watching the animatronic dinosaur swish its tail back and forth, and whipping her booty back and forth in solidarity.

I would have missed the riveting intellectual disagreement between her and her four-year-old cousin about whether an animal was a worm or a snake. (Neither. It was a lizard.) And I would have missed a plastic tub of popcorn, an elephant tumbler full of lemonade, and the opportunity to experience my daughter connecting with a few of her favorite things.

So don't worry, car. True, we're not as tidy as we used to be. But we're living a life full of elephants, dinosaurs, worm-lizards, and adventure. And it's worth this minor sacrifice.

YEAR 3 | DAY 105

I often let my daughter choose a juice when she joins me on grocery runs. Tonight she chose Iron Man, though she has no idea who he is.

Her: Why is he so *mad*?!

Me: He's not mad. That's just a mask. He's a superhero!

Her: But he's a little bit scary…?

Me: Yeah, scary to bad guys! But he likes to help people!

Her: Well, he needs to calm down!

Wise words.

LISTENING

YEAR 3 | DAY 122

Just bought our daughter glow-in-the-dark stars for her bedroom ceiling.

Husband: Is she crying in her room?

Me: Nope, she's howling at the moon.

YEAR 3 | DAY 123

Hungry at 11:00 PM in my 20s: out for cheesesteaks and drinks

Hungry at 11:00 PM in my 30s: *Paw Patrol* string cheese

I've officially mastered the fine art of dressing my 3-year-old while holding her arm the entire time to prevent escape.

YEAR 3 | DAY 131

If you enjoy waiting 15 minutes for a 3-year-old to decide whether she wants blueberries or carrots for her school snack, you would love being a parent. Like, *love*.

YEAR 3 | DAY 137

Bedtime at 2 years old:
1. Cuddle for 20 minutes
2. Good night

Bedtime at 3 years old:
1. Cuddle for 20 minutes
2. "Belly cuddle" (laying on Daddy's chest – a wise delay tactic) for 10 minutes
3. Select a stuffed animal to sleep with
4. Select a book to sleep with
5. Story time with Momma
6. Pray for every person, animal, and stuffed animal that ever lived or will live (another wise delay tactic – how do you say no to prayers?)
7. Beg Momma to cuddle for a minute
8. As Momma is leaving, announce you *must* poop now, insist you didn't have to poop 40 minutes ago
9. Sit on toilet for 10 minutes, not pooping
10. Good night

Send help.

YEAR 3 | DAY 146

Today I was invited to a "picnic" in the hallway. My daughter "shopped" for the food in her room, hand-selected our dishes, and packed it all into her grocery basket. Then she escorted me down the hall, where she had carefully spread out her superhero cape for us, turned off the lights, and made firework sounds as we shared plastic pineapples and fries together.

For all of the hard days and nights I've counted down the hours to bedtime, for all of the times I've lost my patience and said and done things I've regretted, she still planned every detail of a special picnic for me.

We beat ourselves up as parents, wishing we did more of one thing, less of another. We read blog posts about cherishing every moment, never lifting our phones or averting our attention, then feel like failures when we take a moment for ourselves.

But our kids don't see any of that. They just see that we love them and that they can count on us to be there for them. While we're busy condemning ourselves, they're making sure they pack plastic ice cream, because they know it's our favorite.

So don't be so hard on yourself, momma. *You are a good parent.* Just ask your kids.

YEAR 3 | DAY 167

Just allowed my three-year-old to eat clementines, a spoonful of peanut butter, and a few chocolate-covered almonds for dinner...if you were wondering how our day is going.

YEAR 3 | DAY 177

Items my child packed for a sleepover tonight:

- Her Halloween costume
- A pumpkin
- Her acorn collection

Items my child did not pack for her sleepover:

- Pajamas
- Toothbrush
- Sleeping bag

LISTENING

YEAR 3 | DAY 180

My husband and I just returned from a short weekend getaway in Dallas. We stayed at a swanky hotel, wandered around Uptown, caught up with a few friends, and saw Bruno Mars perform. (Ah-mazing!) And I was reminded of those carefree days before I was a mother.

...when I didn't have much of a schedule or agenda outside of work hours, and could spring for a nap whenever the mood struck.

...when I didn't have to pack toys to entertain, or download *Daniel Tiger* episodes onto a Kindle, or plan snacks and backup snacks to appeal to my three-year-old's ever-changing mood.

...when I could eat and drink in peace in a restaurant and didn't have to share with anyone or constantly wipe sticky fingers and faces.

And for a moment, it made me feel a little wistful for those carefree days.

But the very next moment, I was missing my girl. I missed cuddling and praying with her before bed. I missed making her snacks and watching her happily "share" them with her stuffed animals. I missed her climbing onto my lap to try a bite of my meal after she swore she would eat her own this time.

Getaways are nice. They allow me to reconnect with my husband and take a break from the constant mental load that weighs on me at home. But they also always remind me that the work is so worth it.

That tiny human, though she comes with a boatload of responsibility and stress, completes our lives. Her very existence injects more weight and meaning into every word we speak, every action we take, and every decision we make.

Sure, life used to be easier. But the best things in life always require a fight. And our children are worth that fight. They're worth the frustration, the exhaustion, the long days and tears and tantrums. They're worth our time and energy and love.

So take a break. (You deserve one!) But when you're back in the thick of things, remember that the best things in life always require a fight. And they're *worth* fighting for. You've got this!

LISTENING

YEAR 3 | DAY 184

Dinner time, eating stew.

Me to three-year-old: And what do vegetables do?! (expecting a "Make you big and strong!")

Three-year-old: Turn into poo poo!

YEAR 3 | DAY 186

Last night, as we were brushing her teeth, my daughter looked up at me and smiled. "I love doing fun things with you," she happily declared.

"Brushing your teeth is fun?!" I asked with a laugh.

"Yeah! It's so much fun!"

We work so hard to create these magical memories for our kids and feel like the more elaborate the plans, the more time and money we spend, the more our kids will love it. And yet, here's a three-year-old, declaring how much she loves brushing her teeth with her mom. It reminded me not to overlook the little moments, the one-on-one attention and conversation during everyday activities.

Maybe we don't have to work so hard to create special memories for our children. Maybe we're making them every day...eating dinner...laughing together...even brushing our teeth.

YEAR 3 | DAY 200

This morning started with me cutting fruit to pack in my daughter's preschool snack while she rolled around the floor, demanding that I retrieve her toy (which she had just thrown across the kitchen in frustration, by the way), then pausing to cry when I didn't. Back and forth, demanding to crying.

It didn't last long. She shaped up and started her day well. But it reminded me of what I read in the Bible this morning.

"No doubt about it! God is good...But I nearly missed it, missed seeing His goodness. I was looking the other way" (Psalm 73:1-2). In this chapter in Psalms, David wrote that he almost missed seeing God's goodness to *him* because he was too busy envying others and looking at what *they* had.

I thought of how my daughter was so caught up in demanding that I give her a toy, that she was completely oblivious to the fact I was preparing something else for her. She wasn't thinking about her snack, didn't make the connection that it was something she'd need and want in the future (like, an *hour* in the future), and only saw her current situation.

When you're laying on the floor with tears in your eyes, it's hard to see what's developing on the kitchen counter. You're both physically and emotionally incapable of seeing the bigger picture.

This morning, I was reminded that God is *good*, and to trust in His goodness. I have zero intentions of not meeting my daughter's every need and then some. And sometimes I deny her certain things because I know they'll hurt her in the long run or distract her from the better option.

But in the end, she *will* be provided for in the best way possible. When she's older, she'll be able to see the bigger picture...and she'll understand.

So if you're crying on the floor this morning, remember to look up. Don't look the other way. Don't get too lost in your tears.

God is working this very moment to meet your needs. You just might not be able to see it yet. *Yet.*

YEAR 3 | DAY 201

Just untangled a string cheese wrapper from my daughter's hair because #momlife.

YEAR 3 | DAY 236

Sorry we were late. My daughter had to finish cooking and serving a meal to stuffed animals, lament for a few minutes that she couldn't wear her favorite shirt for a third day, make an agonizing sock decision, get dressed all by herself, and find the "perfect" leaf in our treeless yard, all before entering the car.

YEAR 3 | DAY 237

'Tis the season of my child yelling "It's Santa!" at every passing white-bearded old man.

YEAR 3 | DAY 241

It's almost Christmas and I'm running through a mental checklist to make sure my child has:

✓ Visited Santa

✓ Experienced a holiday lights display

✓ Decorated a gingerbread house

...and all of the other wholesome, memorable traditions we feel we need to check off our list to be good Hallmark Channel parents over the holidays.

Meanwhile, my daughter received new markers from her papa and nana, and has spent the evening furiously drawing every member of our family and hanging the pictures up throughout the house.

Everyone looked pretty much the same except for one picture, a stick person surrounded by what looked like messy chicken pecks. I asked her who it was and she told me it was her. I asked what all of the dots around her were. She was the only one that had them.

Know what they were? My kisses.

Of all the activities we've checked off our list the last few weeks, she didn't draw a single one. She wasn't thinking of activities and extravagant traditions when she thought of her family. She was thinking of kisses, of the love of her mother.

Our kids don't need more activities each holiday season. They just need our love, our time, our attention... our kisses.

So go easy on yourself when holidays arrive. I honestly believe our kids don't want events and crafts and elves and *things* half as much as they want us.

Stay present. Stay in the moment, even if the moment isn't extravagant or exciting or Pinterest-worthy. Your love is what's making memories.

YEAR 3 | DAY 242

Heard a fart come out of my daughter this afternoon… then a long pause…then, with a sad sigh, "This house smells bad. We're gonna have to get a new one now." Sounds about right.

YEAR 3 | DAY 246

Me to daughter: No, sorry, you can't eat a cheese danish in your car seat.

Husband: Oh, come on! Just let her enjoy it!

Husband (15 minutes later in the car): What?! *No! Nooooo!!*

CHAPTER 3 | LEARNING

Today I finally cleaned my entire house top to bottom from the chaos of Christmas...then I let my 3-year-old eat peanut butter for dinner. It's called balance.

LEARNING

YEAR 3 | DAY 263

I am *struggling* to cook anything since the holidays. So today, we ate a pre-made grocery store salad topped with pre-cooked and shredded grocery store chicken for dinner. And my daughter (still wearing her Halloween costume in January) told me, "Mom, I *love* your cooking!" I'm taking this as my cue to give up cooking forever.

Motherhood: Getting out in public without your kids, starting to feel all young and hip, then finding a Paw Patrol string cheese wrapper in your coat pocket.

YEAR 3 | DAY 267

Her: Wanna be in my band?

Me: I don't play an instrument.

Her: Do you know how to play a dinosaur trumpet?

Me: A dinosaur...trumpet?

Her: Hold on, I'll make you one. (jams a kazoo on the end of a plastic dinosaur's tail)

YEAR 3 | DAY 279

My three-year-old is currently drowning in mucus and the conversation on repeat goes something like this:

Her: It's in my throat! How do I get it out?
Me: I have to suck it out with the NoseFrida.
Her: No!
Me: It's the only way to help, babe!
Her: No, I don't like that.
Me: So you're just gonna be sad and keep it in your nose?
Her: Yeah.

I'm not exaggerating when I say we've had this exact conversation 20 times in the past 2 days. Meanwhile, she keeps yelling, "my nose!" every few minutes. And we wipe her nose knowing it's not what she *really* needs.

Now I don't let a three-year-old call the shots. I've used the NoseFrida several times a day anyway and she always feels much better after.

But our conversation has made me think about how I often speak with God.

Me: I'm in trouble! How do I fix it?
God: I can fix it, but it's going to be uncomfortable.
Me: No!
God: It's the only way to truly *fix* it and make you whole.
Me: No, I don't like that!
God: So you're just gonna be sad and stay in that trouble?

Me: Yeah.

We want God to fix things for us but we want him to do it *our* way. But sometimes (in fact, *most* of the time!) the path to true and lasting healing hurts.

Sometimes it requires us to change long-established habits. Sometimes it demands we give up something we love for something much better for us. Sometimes it calls us to a long walk through the valley but with the promise of victory, and a better outcome than we could have ever imagined for ourselves, on the other side.

But that sounds hard. It sounds painful. So we say no. And we continue to struggle with the same issues over and over again.

We try throwing other solutions at it.

More support from family and friends!

A miracle diet or supplement!

A better body!

A new job!

A new identity!

More things! Bigger and better things!

More hustle!

More money!

More success!

But if you're anything like me, you've found those are only temporary solutions. They might make you feel better for a while but they always let you down in the end, right back down into the same place you started.

Are you tired of facing the same old issue, dressed up in different ways, day after day? Year after year? Are you exhausted from throwing every idea you've got at it, with nothing working? Nothing sticking?

Take the hard road. Walk where Jesus is pointing, where He's walking ahead of you, and behind you, and right beside you.

It might not be the path you were hoping for. It might even hurt or cost you something. But it's the *only* path to true and lasting healing, to a lasting solution to the issue you're facing. I know from experience.

"God is striding ahead of you. He's right there with you. He won't let you down; He won't leave you. Don't be intimidated. Don't worry" (Deuteronomy 31:8).

I just briefly considered hiding in the bathroom to eat my cheeseburger in peace and quiet...in case you were wondering what it's like to be a parent.

YEAR 3 | DAY 302

Today, we visited the doctor. While we waited in the examination room, my daughter scaled the exam table like it was a mountain, grunting, shouting, and all, then lamented over how she was going to get back down.

Ten billion times, her feet were within inches of the step stool below her. We cheered, "You're almost there, keep going!" But from *her* vantage point, she was a million miles away. So she crawled back up, regained her composure, and started all over again.

It reminded me of a quote by Thomas Edison, "Many of life's failures are people who did not realize how close they were to success when they gave up." And I realized in that moment my daughter was a failure. Just kidding!

But it made me wonder how close we might be to victory, just inches from our goal, when we give up. From our vantage point, or looking through the lens of our emotions, we're a million miles away. So we pack our bags and abort mission.

Today, I beg you...don't give up! You might be one more workout from beginning to see the results of your hard work...one more sale from making a real career of this new venture...one more assignment from passing that class from hell (I'm looking at you, kinesiology!), just one more prayer from your breakthrough.

Don't allow your emotions, or your exhaustion, to call the shots. If it matters to you, I mean *really* matters, keep going! You might just be inches away from your victory.

YEAR 3 | DAY 313

I had a plan:

1. Go inside.
2. Wind my daughter down for a nap.
3. Kick butt on work the second her head hit the pillow.

Then my daughter wasn't ready to go inside. Then she was hungry. Then she wanted to open the garage door, set up chairs, and pretend she was camping as she ate her Lunchable.

I sighed. And then I decided...meh, why not? And instead of rushing off to check things off my list, I just sat in the 70° garage (Thank you, Texas!), watched her start with her cookie (as always), and chatted about her time in the park that morning with Grandma and Grandpa.

And you know what? I think this kid is onto something. It was just the mental break I needed.

Just sit today...not in front of a screen...not in front of a task that needs doing. Just...sit...breathe...be. Who knows? It might just be what you need, too.

Just realized my almost 4-year-old has been hearing "pie school" any time someone says "high school" and I have so many questions.

YEAR 3 | DAY 315

"If you don't calm down, I'm gonna take away your crowbar." – things I apparently say now that my child has a toy firefighter set

YEAR 3 | DAY 324

Me: What should we wear to school today?

Three-year-old: ...(long pause, lots of serious thought)...a mustache!

In case you were wondering why we're never on time.

LEARNING

YEAR 3 | DAY 342

Running out of date night ideas? Here's a fun one!

Wake up in the middle of the night to the sound of a dead smoke detector battery. Work frantically to locate the beeping detector, find a 9-volt battery, and replace it before it wakes up your 3-year-old and you're doomed to a night of being kicked in the head.

Gotta keep things spicy!

YEAR 3 | DAY 345

A packed trash can with a paper towel carefully stretched across the top is the international sign for: I might have gone through your mountain of art projects and thrown a few away. Please don't look in here.

One day, I'd love to be as patient and calm as the Man in the Yellow Hat. Your monkey just hijacked a hot air balloon and is floating to certain death? "Oh, boy."

YEAR 3 | DAY 353

Child wakes up extra early, crawls into my bed, and lays quietly in my arms.

Me (thinking): Well, *this* is a pleasant surprise.

Child starts yodeling.

Me: *There* it is!

YEAR 3 | DAY 357

Three-year-old: (tells me the story of Easter)

Me: (heart swells with joy, eyes well up with tears)

Three-year-old: And there were lots of sharks, and they bit his feet!

Me: Wait...what?!

YEAR 3 | DAY 363

Her: I drew you, Mom!

Me: Aw, I love it! Am I making a peace sign?!

Her: No, it's a pizza sign.

Me: Are you sure it's not a *peace* sign?

Her: Yeah! Look, it looks like a piece of pizza.

Valid point...

LEARNING

YEAR 4 | DAY 3

I returned to full-time work just over a month ago, my first time to work away from home in four years. I also act as my daughter's primary caregiver for roughly 7 hours every weekday (and all day weekends), and spend 10-15 hours a week writing and editing for my own website and others. To say that I have to mindfully manage every *single* minute is an obvious understatement.

Any time I sit down on the couch instead of tending to dishes – guilt. Any time I take a nap or call a friend instead of writing during my daughter's nap – guilt. I tell myself I only have so much time, and it's true.

But this morning, I found a faster route to work that landed me there 25 minutes earlier. And as I began to gather my things to run inside to write or maybe finalize plans for my daughter's birthday party, I decided instead to take the morning off.

And so, in the middle of a quiet parking lot, enveloped by gray, dreary skies and a light mist of rain, I simply sat in my car and watched an actor's interview on my phone. I laughed and laughed again, deep belly laughs, and kept laughing throughout my morning as I remembered things said.

No, I didn't check another item off my list in those 25 minutes. And I certainly didn't accomplish anything worthy of a #girlboss status. I simply gave something I sincerely enjoyed my full attention for a few minutes. And to be honest? It was the most refreshing 25 minutes of my entire week.

We all have a lot on our plates, and *it's okay* if we don't utilize *every* second to accomplish a task. Don't allow false guilt to trick you into believing otherwise.

Slow down today. Rest. Refresh. Reset. The rest of your day will still be there when you're done.

YEAR 4 | DAY 14

Four-year-old: Mom, can we watch Giantman in the living room?

Me: Who's Giantman?

Four-year-old: (proceeds to describe Giantman, even drawing a picture of him, for 10 *minutes*)

Me: I have *no* idea, babe! Where have you seen Giantman?

Four-year-old: My son watched it.

Me: ...your...pretend son?

Four-year-old: My son. On the TV in my room.

Me: ...you don't have a TV in your room.

Four-year-old: Right. I have a movie theater in my room. That's where we watched Giantman. I played it for him.

Me: Yeeeeeah, I don't have any of the movies that are in your head. Just...actual...movies.

Four-year-old: (yelling down the hall to her room) Sorry, son! They don't have that movie on their TV!

And this is why you should always clarify questions with a preschooler before going down the rabbit hole...

Wishing you didn't have to set your alarm clock tonight? Birth a child. All your wildest dreams will come true!

YEAR 4 | DAY 51

"Ugh, I can't do anything when the dog keeps getting in my way!" she says.

"That must be super hard," I say, as I attempt to blow dry my hair without blowing her crayons across the bathroom floor.

YEAR 4 | DAY 72

Four-year-old: I'm gonna put on a play for you! Do you want...Platypus Knows Everything? Or There's Nothing in My Closet to Wear?

Decisions, decisions...

YEAR 4 | DAY 89

Forget jail time. They should trap criminals in a room with a pack of kids. And every time they fall asleep, the kids jump on their spleen and ask something like, "Why can't turtles talk?!" until they're reformed.

My work here is done.

LEARNING

YEAR 4 | DAY 90

I had what seemed like a genius idea today – to work on my writing at my favorite coffee shop...with my four-year-old. She said she'd love to "get some work done with me," and as I packed up my MacBook and planner, she carefully packed a coloring book, crayons, dog book, parachute man, and of course, her Chase stuffy. Because *Paw Patrol* is life.

When we arrived, we chose the perfect seat and ordered a latte, a hot chocolate with whipped cream and sprinkles, and a huge cookie to share. I opened my MacBook and finished roughly 30 seconds of work before I realized it was all a pipe dream. The very same child who *swore* she wanted to color and read just 10 minutes earlier, now wanted nothing more than to chat with her momma.

I had hoped to get ahead of my schedule for once, instead of always falling two steps behind. I wanted to finish writing a post and to schedule out social media for the coming week.

But if I would have stubbornly held onto my original plans, insisting on them despite the obvious turn of events, I would have missed out...on my daughter proudly sharing her artwork...or inviting me to a slow dance...or hard-core cheesing, yelling, "Say hot cocoaaaaa!" when we snapped a quick selfie together.

And I've decided that's really the secret sauce to life. Set a goal, make your plans, but when your plans fall to pieces? Just breathe in the moment you're in. It's all you

111

have anyway, so you might as well make the most of every moment, whether it's the moment you planned or another one altogether.

LEARNING

YEAR 4 | DAY 93

Her: Mom, should I color this red or green or blue?

Me: Red.

Her: No.

Me: Green.

Her: No.

Me: Blue.

Her: Oh okay, great choice!

YEAR 4 | DAY 112

We're back home after spending the weekend visiting family in Galveston, Texas. While at the beach, my daughter wanted nothing more than to join her older cousins farther out in the waves. But to get there, we had to push through the breakers – those waves that crash onto the shore in a white foam and feel and hurt like a physical slap to your shins...then thighs...then stomach...until you've finally pushed through them to the more gentle waves.

And those breakers kept pushing us backward. They threatened our balance. They made it seem much easier and simpler to just remain on the shore.

And to be honest, we could have been happy enough on the shore. There were kites and shovels and pails and sandwiches.

But instead, I encouraged my daughter to fight through them. I assured her that with just a few more pushes, we'd reach our destination. And darn, if I didn't feel those words deep in my gut.

Because how many new beginnings start with breakers? We're determined to establish a positive new habit, then fall short by the end of our first day. We get pumped about a new hobby, a passion that could ignite our minds and our hearts and quickly become our new "thing." But then we look around and start comparing ourselves to others and are knocked back down onto our butts on the shoreline.

We decide to finally take that big step...returning to school...launching a new career...leaving what we've known our entire lives...and it doesn't quite turn out like we expected. Those are the breakers, my friend.

And if we allow them to discourage us? To cause us to lose our hope and our strength and return to the shore? Then we'll never experience the joy and satisfaction of reaching our destination – our positive habits, our passions, our careers, our new lives...our older cousins.

Don't let those initial setbacks set *you* back. Recognize them as your breakers and *push through them today*. Because they won't last forever. And they only hold power over you if you let them.

The ocean is calling, friend. Push through to your future.

YEAR 4 | DAY 125

When I was pregnant, I assumed it was my mini-me stretching my belly and kicking me in the ribs. So before she was even born, I had filled my daughter's bookshelf with all of my childhood favorites. I imagined her quietly reading, listening to stories as they were fed to her, asking for instructions to every activity, and following them to a T.

But instead...God gave me an artist. And she had her own take on every project.

Rather than carefully filling the outlined spaces of a coloring page, she added to the picture. When handed the pieces to create an animal or some other straightforward project, she created something entirely different.

And at first, it frustrated me. Do this! Follow these steps! I would instruct her, then bite my tongue at what felt like incompletion. The finished product lacked the satisfaction of looking exactly like the example.

But the more time we spent together, the more I observed her in quiet wonder, the more God used my artist to challenge and stretch me. I began to realize that her way wasn't wrong or incomplete. It was just different...and a heck of a lot more freeing.

She slowly pushed and bent and molded me until I started asking questions like, "Why not? What have I got to lose? Why not try things differently?" And as she grew into herself as an artist, I grew from a reader into a writer...from a consumer into a creator.

Because why limit myself to the stories others are telling? Why not create something of my own? Take a risk? And I've gotta tell you, my life is 110% better for it.

Yes, there are days (most days) that our differences can be frustrating. We butt heads. We lose our patience.

But the lessons we can learn from our less-than-mini-mes? They're worth the hard work and long days and relearning everything we thought we knew.

And those children who are our exact opposites? They're worth the fight. Knowing and understanding and connecting with their hearts is what parenting is all about.

So don't lose hope, fellow parent! These kids are pushing our limits, but they're leaving us better for it.

YEAR 4 | DAY 127

Four-year-old at Walgreens: Can we please buy Snoopy?

Me: Not this time.

Four-year-old: Can I just hold him while you look at cards?

Me: Sure.

Snoopy (starts singing): I used to have a kiiiiid...who loved me and did everything with meeeee...until he found out I was just a stuffy and not a real dog...and he would never love me agaaaaain.

Four-year-old: Wow, that's *so* sad!

Snoopy (singing again): I used to sleep in my kid's bed every niiiiight...now I sleep alone in this stooooore.

- The reason we have 3,774,484 stuffed animals

YEAR 4 | DAY 137

I woke up this morning with a blazing headache. All I wanted to do was stay in bed for an extra hour.

But my daughter? She woke up with a blazing attitude. Because of course. She pouted, grimaced, and flopped onto the floor in exasperation.

I tried everything I could to help her settle her frustrations without leaving my bed. I asked what was wrong. I suggested things that might cheer her up. I even tried asking in the dog's voice when my own voice wasn't doing the trick.

I considered yelling. Of course. I stomped my feet in my own tantrum in my head.

But then I thought about all of the mornings *I've* woken up with a bad attitude and couldn't quite pinpoint the cause. I understood. So instead, I sent her to choose a snack from the pantry and turned on *Curious George*.

While she quietly munched beside me, I thought through 10 million things I could say to her, 10 million tough lessons that could be taught in that moment. Finally, I made a very serious face, looked her in the eyes, and said... "I want you to know something. I love you, even when you're grumpy. When you're happy, I love you. But when you're grumpy? I love you just as much." I wish you could have seen the warmth of the smile that spread across her small face.

No, it didn't transform her into a perfect angel. Yes, I'll have to continue disciplining her for years to come.

But the fact is that God loves us just as much on our worst day as He does on our best. And if we're not imparting that same message to our children, if we're not occasionally demonstrating that grace, who will?

And how will they know at the core of their being when they're older that their rough starts, their shortcomings, and their failures don't define them? How will they learn to show themselves grace?

Sure, send them to timeout. Take away their phone. Do what you need to discipline them, but be sure to deliver this truth right alongside it.

Because it's much harder to believe and embrace when you're older. But we already know that, don't we?

YEAR 4 | DAY 152

Her: Hey mom, let's pretend I'm a boy and I jam and you like me. (Steps out onto a "stage," plays a few strokes on her ukulele, and walks over to me dripping with confidence) Hi.

Me: Hi. What's your name?

Her: Jam. Cuz I like to jam. You wanna go to a fancy restaurant and eat dinner? Then we can have a sleepover every night forever?

Me: Um…

Her: But I'm gonna need you to buy me a car. I just have a scooter.

Guys. I have no words.

YEAR 4 | DAY 179

Yesterday was a hard day. It was my four-year-old's first day back at preschool after fighting off sickness, and a longer day at that.

Sure, she seemed happy when we picked her up, clutching the hand of her best friend and grinning from ear to ear. But then we had to hurry...we rushed her through choosing a book from the lending library and couldn't stop to say goodbye to her friend for the eighth time.

And it all went downhill from there. All of her exhaustion and frustration swept in like a tidal wave, leaving her in tears, unable to communicate beyond wails.

Her dad and I told her to take deep breaths. We told her to use her words. We tried explaining. We tried threatening. But each word out of our mouths only seemed to feed her agony.

When she was an infant, I spent *hours* with my arm stretched back into her carseat, her tiny hand tightly clutching my numb and tingling fingers. And so yesterday, when neither my words nor hers seemed adequate to remedy the situation, I simply reached out to hold her hand in silence.

Her breathing began to slow. Her wails fell to a whimper. I told her about how she liked to hold my hand like this when she was little. I explained how my arm would ache, but she would cry when I let go, so I'd keep reaching, keep holding.

And she smiled at the story. She wanted to hear more.

Sometimes our kids don't need words. Words couldn't serve or dispel their frustrations anyway. They simply need a hand to hold, someone to sit with them in the moment until the feelings pass.

Don't our actions speak louder than our words anyway?

Current hormone level: Ugly crying at the end of Toy Story 3

Sorry we were late, we had to find hats for our Lego people so they weren't too cold in the car.

YEAR 4 | DAY 185

Currently trying to catch a five-minute nap while my foot is being used as a "rope" to save my kid from "falling off a cliff" and this pretty much sums up parenthood.

YEAR 4 | DAY 190

Four-year-old: Can you please watch these dinosaurs while I ride my bike? They're in love, so just make sure they don't do...you know...the disgusting things dinosaurs do when they're in love.

I *don't* know. But I'm too afraid to ask...

YEAR 4 | DAY 195

Every year, my daughter's preschool hosts a gingerbread house fundraiser. Last year, I offered to help by cutting and baking some pre-made dough at home.

But I quickly learned that rolling dough to a specific and uniform width is not actually in my wheelhouse. Nor is making it look pretty.

So this year, I volunteered to make the dough itself. They had pre-measured and labeled the ingredients and just needed some volunteers to mix it.

So I lugged my stand mixer to the preschool over my lunch break, plugged it in, aaaand realized the paddle wasn't reaching the ingredients in the bowl. After awkwardly attempting to hold the bowl closer using my hands, I mentioned my "strange" issue to the mom beside me. She turned the (very obvious) crank to raise the bowl. I hadn't used my mixer since my daughter was born. I guess I forgot the crank part.

It also turns out that if you mix gingerbread dough too fast, it will fly out of the bowl and fling itself across the room. Just ask those standing near me. Also, dumping it out of the bowl too quickly will shoot it past the parchment paper and onto the floor.

Even as I lugged my mixer to the sink to wash it after we'd finished, I somehow stepped on the back of my *own* shoe and took it clean off my foot. But I couldn't bend over to grab it while carrying my mixer. So I left it there to come back for later.

I am not a Food Network-caliber baker. Obviously. And you know what? That's totally okay.

My daughter may never have perfect gingerbread houses, like the kid of the mom expertly mixing two batches at once next to me. But she *does* have a mother who slays all day managing a team, digging through reporting, and streamlining processes at the office.

She has a mom who relentlessly pursues her passions, is involved in her church and community, and invests one-on-one time with her daughter for the first seven hours of the day, before starting an eight-hour workday that ends at midnight. She has a mother who is insightful, strong, patient, and most importantly, understands and loves her daughter for exactly who she is.

We all have different strengths and gifts. And if we spend all of our time and energy beating ourselves up and pining over others' gifts, we might miss out on discovering the very special gifts God has hidden in *us*.

It's okay if you don't have certain gifts. Explore and utilize the gifts you *do* have. And help your kids to discover and develop and celebrate their *own* gifts. That's the gift that will keep on giving, even after they've grown too old for gingerbread houses.

CHAPTER 4 | ADJUSTING

YEAR 4 | DAY 199

Her: Can I watch a movie?

Me: Sure, what do you want?

Her: *Tree Stand.*

Me: *Tree...Stand?*

Her: Yeah.

Me: What's it about?

Her: These kids are trying to help a tree stand so he can be like all the other trees, but he keeps falling over.

Me: ...

Her: ...

Me: Is that a movie in your head?

Her: Yeah.

Me: I meant what movie on Hulu.

Her: Oh.

ADJUSTING

YEAR 4 | DAY 235

It's Christmas Eve morning and I have so many things to do...prep our breakfast for tomorrow morning, vacuum, fold the towels that have been sitting in the dryer for nearly a week now, and more. But then...of course...my daughter asked me to sit next to her while she tried out a new Christmas gift, an art set, at the kitchen table.

"Can I fold towels beside you while you draw?"

"No, I just want you to sit with me."

And if the tasks on my to-do list were essential, I might have had to tell her to wait (which I often do). But I realized she won't notice if the floor is mostly clean or extra clean when she sits near the tree to open her gifts tomorrow. And she won't know if I grabbed her towel from a neatly folded stack in the hall closet or from a crumpled pile atop the dryer. And breakfast prep for the next day? It probably doesn't *have* to happen before 10:00 am today.

And so I'm sitting...and watching...and learning the names of all her favorite people in her drawing. And I believe *this* is what my daughter will remember...a lazy Christmas Eve morning, drawing quietly with her momma.

So go easy on yourself today! And focus your time and energy on the things they *will* remember. Merry Christmas!

YEAR 4 | DAY 251

"I'm a lion but I'm a nice lion. My parents like to bite people until they die, but I just want to invite you to my party!" - my four-year-old's disturbing description of the lion she drew today

ADJUSTING

YEAR 4 | DAY 265

So here's a fun tradition we started last year – every holiday, unleash your child on a dollar store to decorate their room for the holiday. It costs me $5-6 max, feels like a wild shopping spree to my 4-year-old, and leaves her *so* full of joy every time she steps into her room.

YEAR 4 | DAY 279

Do you ever take pictures from your vantage point? Photos that capture what something looks like from your exact position in that moment? I highly recommend it.

When my daughter was first born, I captured a few photos of what it looked like from my point of view looking down on her as she breastfed or slept on my chest. As she's grown older, I've sneaked photos of my view of the top of her head as she's snuggled into me to watch a movie...or after she and a couch pillow weasel their way into my bed on a lazy Saturday morning.

"You'll miss these days." That's what they say. And so I take pictures to help me remember what it looked and felt like feeding and snuggling my daughter while she was still small...and waking up to find her in my bed.

Try it! I guarantee they'll be some of your favorite, most treasured photos when your children are older.

I learn something new every day. For example, if someone offers your child their leftover sequins, the correct answer is apparently, "No, thank you!"

YEAR 4 | DAY 341

We've been getting outside more lately, taking walks together every morning. And from the very beginning, I was thinking of our walks as a chance for fresh air and exercise, a healthy duty to hurry and check off my list.

But my daughter? She freezes dramatically as she catches sight of a mushroom, asks a hundred curious questions about the pine needles scattered across the sidewalk, and marvels at the beauty in an otherwise ordinary tree. She demands that we take pictures to capture what she considers to be small miracles.

And you know what? She's right. They are. During a time that most of us are trying to simply survive each day juggling work, childcare, errands, and more, let's not miss out on the hundreds of small miracles that God is performing just for us every day.

ADJUSTING

YEAR 4 | DAY 345

I've started working from home...

Me: You can't talk to me right now.

Four-year-old: Is it okay if I have hiccups?

Me: That's fine.

Four-year-old: What if there's a fire? Can I tell you there's a fire?

Send help.

YEAR 4 | DAY 351

Me purchasing a cup of caterpillars and butterfly habitat: This is an educational opportunity for my four-year-old.

Me two weeks later: OH MY GOSH, THEY'RE HATCHIIIIING!!

I made you this special ninja water. It will make your kicks stronger and your karate chops faster.

- lies that work

YEAR 5 | DAY 1

This is motherhood.

It's braving Walmart in a mask to pick up a few party supplies when your kid's fifth birthday lands in the middle of a quarantine.

It's getting off work at midnight, then immediately shifting gears to start decorating your kitchen.

It's groaning as you lower your tired body to the floor to place a trail of paper paw prints down the hall. And it's smiling to yourself with each paw print you place because you already know the exact face she'll make when she discovers them.

This is motherhood.

It's feeling completely exhausted and so full of joy in the very same moment. It's willingly giving up your own time, energy, and money for your children because they're your favorite way to spend your time, energy, and money.

This is motherhood.

It requires *everything* of you, but somehow takes what you give, mashes it down, and gives you back much more than you ever had in the first place.

This is motherhood. And this is my favorite place to be.

YEAR 5 | DAY 20

These are the hard nights.

They're the nights when long, trying days and thunderstorms mean middle-of-the-night awakenings and endless, inconsolable tears. They're the nights when making little bodies comfortable means letting go of any chance of your own comfort, the nights your heart sinks as you watch the clock count down hours of potential sleep.

But when she looks back on these nights, my daughter won't remember the sheer exhaustion and sleeplessness. No, she'll remember the warmth of her mother's arms, the safety she felt in her parents' bed, the comfort of being loved completely and unconditionally, even in the most trying of circumstances.

And that's the knowledge that drives me forward. These long nights won't last forever for us. They're a passing phase, a blip in a bigger timeline.

But these nights? They'll last forever in our children's hearts. They'll build a foundation of love and safety that will last a lifetime.

Hang in there, momma. You're doing deeply meaningful work tonight.

YEAR 5 | DAY 30

My daughter and I grow vegetables on our back patio every spring. And this year, I'm learning more about myself from my pepper plant.

See, my pepper plant is strong. It surprises me with new growth and peppers every morning and despite the weight of a million peppers, stands upright all on its own.

But it's not alone in the planter. It's joined on either side by a cucumber plant and a watermelon plant, both of which reach out tendrils to climb on whatever will support them which in this case, is primarily the pepper plant.

Now the pepper plant can support them for a while, because it's strong. But as more tendrils attach and more vines hang their weight from its branches, even the strong pepper plant begins to bend and nearly break under the added weight.

And so I pull the tendrils off of it. Constantly. If I don't, the pepper plant will eventually break under the weight and be no good to anyone, least of all itself.

You might be a strong person. You might be able to carry all of the weight others place on you. But it doesn't mean you should. Or even that you can!

Sure, support others. Lend an ear and a helping hand, pray for them, write them an encouraging note, drop off some groceries, do whatever you can to support them.

But.

But....*you are not responsible for their growth.* And you are not responsible for their choices.

144

You can support them all day, but when it comes down to it, they have to grow all on their own. They have to make the decision for themselves to take that step forward, to do that hard thing.

Because you're ultimately responsible for growing peppers, not someone else's cucumbers. Just because you can handle the weight of someone else pushing past your personal boundaries and demanding from you what they should demand from themselves, doesn't mean that you should.

Because even though it feels okay right now, you'll break eventually. And you won't just break for them. You'll break for yourself and for other people that need you, too.

Don't be afraid to pull off tendrils today, to set healthy boundaries. You're not being unsupportive. In fact, you're *helping* them. Your boundary-setting might be the thing that pushes them to grow all on their own...and to realize that they *can* grow all on their own.

Stay strong, friend. You've got peppers to grow.

YEAR 5 | DAY 58

I don't question any parent scrolling their phone while their children play. They deserve a break. Heck, they deserve an entire vacation to themselves! After all, I think we can all agree that parenting is a deeply exhausting gig. *But*...sometimes it pays to be present.

Today at my daughter's swim lesson, I opted out of scrolling my phone. Frankly, social media is more stressful than useful right now and I figured there were more beneficial ways to spend 30 minutes.

Instead, I stood just outside the door with her "cheetah" stuffy that she insists on taking everywhere. (Don't bother telling her it's actually a bear, she'll just lecture you on its cheetah-like qualities.)

Cheetah and I stood at the window together and watched every move of her lesson. I looked down at my phone a few times (mostly to text videos to my husband), but always keeping watch for her to turn my way and looking up the second she did.

And I've gotta tell you...it was like watching this fantastic short film, jam-packed with emotional highs and lows. I watched the fear and doubt build in her eyes as her turn approached to jump into the pool all by herself. I spied her panic as she choked up water for a split second, then was overwhelmed with pride as she quickly composed herself, put on a brave face, and climbed back up to try again.

I witnessed her swim completely unassisted to a platform in the pool and back for the first time in her life. And in that moment, I watched her whip around with a smile as bright as the sun to see if I was watching.

And I was.

Our eyes met and shouted a thousand joyous words without making a sound. And I was *so* thankful I chose today to stay present.

I won't always be present. After all, parents do deserve a break. Sometimes we need to pay bills or reply to emails or text back our mothers who *will not stop* until we reply.

And sometimes we just need to zone out on social media. It's absolutely essential that we take regular time to pause and rest.

But I would encourage you to practice being present when you can. Put away distractions and focus for just a few moments on whatever your children (or spouse or friends!) are doing. I promise you'll be thankful you did.

YEAR 5 | DAY 65

We bought a "house bed" (a bed with cute little walls and a roof) two years ago (1) to trick our child into staying in bed (it worked!) and (2) because it was *gorgeous* and magical and very Joanna Gaines-y. And for a while it stayed gorgeous, with perfectly matched bedding.

But then...my daughter got the "coolest *ever*!" dinosaur sleeping bag. She was so in love with it that she begged me to use it instead of her super cute comforter. And she was just so darn excited that I said yes.

Then...Spider-Man. She loved, loved, *loved* Spider-Man. And when she received a Spider-Man pillow for Christmas, she asked me, "You know what would look *amazing* with my dinosaur sleeping bag?!...*a Spider-Man pillow!*" Goodbye, adorable woodland theme!

Then the art started. I was going on a work trip, so she insisted we draw a few pictures together and hang them up on the inside walls of her "house bed" so that she could look at them while I was gone. And then the art just kept coming.

At first they were scattered about here and there, mostly hand drawn pictures of people and animals following a similar style and theme. Then it was outer space. Then it was coloring pictures of her favorite superheroes and cartoon characters, all piled on top of each other.

And now here we are...in a room with no real theme or cohesive design, scotch taping new pictures up every day, and balancing tiny plastic bags of pirate gold next to pipe cleaner "sculptures" in the windows because "*Wow*, that's so cool!"

Does it match the rest of our home? Definitely not.

Would I prefer a cohesive theme with softer colors and fewer cartoon characters? Yep!

This bed is *not* magazine-worthy. But it conveys my daughter's personality *perfectly*. And just a glance at it lights up her face so much I swear it sparkles.

It's her masterpiece. And I sure as heck am not going to hinder an artist's work.

Yes, I would still love to have my Joanna Gaines-y, dream home. And maybe one day I will.

But she's only this age once. So for now, I'll let her enjoy her dream room.

YEAR 5 | DAY 66

Me (watching a movie with my five-year-old): That's a typewriter. People used those to write before we had computers!

Five-year-old: Yeah, and before that it was feathers with ink. Was it hard to find feathers to write with when you were a kid, Mom?

ADJUSTING

YEAR 5 | DAY 79

Me (tenderly touching my daughter's face): Look at this precious face.

Daughter: I can't see my face...because I'm wearing it...but thanks.

YEAR 5 | DAY 83

Me (waiting on Ninja Turtles to get adopted and meet their new families before my 5-year-old will release me from her 45-minute-long play): Babe, I *have* to start making lunch. This is the longest play I've ever seen!

Her: This is *not* a play.

Me: This is the longest real-life scenario I've ever seen.

Her: I know, right?! Crazy!

Send help.

*Edited to add: It finally ended with Spider-Gwen patting her adopted turtle's head, singing "Beautiful Boy" to him and the dog she surprised him with as they fell asleep together.

ADJUSTING

YEAR 5 | DAY 91

Well, friends, the search is over! I have found the most torturous thing to teach your child and it is...(drumroll, please)...skateboarding!

I was hoping to sit on the curb and watch today, iced coffee in hand. Instead, I found myself walking slowly beside my daughter while she leaned her full weight into me, stretching my favorite shirt as she grabbed and grasped at me to catch her balance on a nearly 100° day. (Does heat make anyone else instantly angry? Asking for a friend...)

Even more torturous than the heat and the clinging was attempting to navigate her rollercoaster of emotions. After all, learning something new is frustrating for adults, let alone five-year-olds.

She would jump and cheer, her entire face lighting up when she mastered a new skill and I would think to myself, "Thank goodness! We're finally getting it! Now where'd I put my coffee?..."

But then the skateboard would escape her control just a moment later, and she'd stomp and scowl and angrily plop her small frame onto the curb.

Le sigh. Parenting is exhausting.

So why did I continue to suffer in the Texas heat even though I was sweaty and thirsty and wanted to stomp and scowl myself? Because I'm helping my five-year-old lay a foundation for her future endeavors. I'm helping lay a super annoying, completely exhausting foundation.

Because this won't be the last new thing she tries. This won't be the last time she fails. And it certainly won't be the last time her anger and frustration make her want to give up altogether.

So today, I'm quietly walking beside her to act as her support. Today, I'm sitting with her in her frustrations on the curb. Today, I'm telling her about when I learned to skateboard and how very badly I sucked at first.

I'm sharing what helped me. And when she's not receptive to what I have to say, I'm sharing it a different way. And sometimes, I'm saying nothing at all except that I'm there for whatever she needs.

And today...she learned to jump onto her skateboard from the ground *and* the curb. Today she steadied her stance.

Today I witnessed complete amazement and pride spread across her face as she accomplished what two minutes ago she believed was impossible. Today she skated down our cul-de-sac as she sang a modified *Daniel Tiger* song – "It takes time, it takes time, to feel like a skateboarding kiiiiid."

This part of parenting is hard. If I'm being honest, it sucks. It's frustrating and exhausting and makes me feel as if I've just finished running a marathon for the rest of the day.

But this is the part that's establishing the baseline effort and discipline and resilience and self-control in our children. And it would be a true disservice to them if we didn't stick out these hot days because we were too annoyed.

So here I am…delaying my coffee and googling skateparks. Because *my* efforts, *your* efforts? They matter.

How is it that my brunette hairs take 22 years to grow out, but my gray hairs can grow 2 inches overnight?

YEAR 5 | DAY 98

Convinced my five-year-old to play "drawing surprise" today, where everyone "pretends to sleep" and dream about what she must be drawing, then she "pretends" to wake us up and surprise us with her completed picture.

Parenting level: 1,000,000

My daughter just chose a vanilla shake over chocolate and I can't believe I brought this monster into the world.

ADJUSTING

YEAR 5 | DAY 100

Last year, my daughter built a small bird house in a Home Depot workshop. We knew absolutely *nothing* about birds, but here was this bird house. So we bought a huge bag of birdseed, poured some into the house, and waited.

Nothing.

Several months later, we decided that maybe we just needed a different bird house. So we bought a new house, hung it from the playscape in the backyard, and waited.

Nothing.

Or so we thought. I mean, we never saw a single bird show interest in it, despite constantly watching it from inside our home.

A few months ago, we decided to move the bird house closer to our back porch, thinking maybe the birds didn't like being so close to where a five-year-old jumped and banged around all day. And lo and behold, when we took down the bird house to move it, we found nests inside.

After we moved the birdhouse next to the back porch, my daughter and I noticed a cardinal begin to frequent the house. When my daughter's gigi informed us that some say cardinals are visitors from heaven, we decided we wanted him to stay. So we dug out the bag of birdseed from the year before and spread some on the porch to see what would happen.

We watched for days. Nothing.

But then...the cardinal visited our porch. Then his family joined him. Then we decided they needed a proper feeder and hung one in a place where we could watch it from our dining room table, where we often find ourselves gathered.

Today, just a few months later, our "bird restaurant" is filled up every single morning and completely emptied by the end of the day. It is frequented by cardinals, finches, juncos, and more, the names of which we've learned from the back of the birdseed bag.

My point is this: Sometimes you're putting in the work, but not yet seeing results. And dang, if it isn't discouraging.

Maybe you're making healthy choices every day, but the scale isn't yet rewarding your efforts. Maybe you're investing time every week into building your business, but so far the rewards are coming up short. Heck, maybe you're praying every day for a friend or family member, but have yet to see the answer to your prayers.

Regardless of what it is you're sowing into right now, *your efforts are not in vain.*

Read that again.

Every healthy choice you make, every minute you invest into reaching your goal, every single word you pray? They're adding up.

You may not see it yet. You may assume your birdhouse is empty. But it's not.

You may not see the cardinal on your porch yet. But if you'd look into the trees past your backyard, you'd see he's getting closer to your house every day.

"Do not despise these small beginnings, for the LORD rejoices to see the work begin" (Zechariah 4:10). And as Lysa TerKeurst once said, "Big things are built one brick at a time."

Your time is coming, friend. Keep taking those steps, no matter how small. Keep watching. You'll be a bird restaurateur soon enough.

YEAR 5 | DAY 107

Tonight my daughter worked her butt off on chores. It was all her idea.

She cleared the kitchen table of every last crayon and colored pencil, picked up every toy from the floor (and even put them back where they belonged), agonized over determining the perfect position for the tissue box, and lamented that I wouldn't allow her to load the dishwasher (tonight's load required Olympic-caliber *Tetris* skills).

She ran up to my desk as I sorted through spreadsheets at work to recount every chore she had completed, offered to do my laundry and give me a "massnage" (massage, haha), and begged me to think of something else she could do. I commended her efforts and marveled at the size of the muscles she said she had built just in the last hour from her cleaning.

Then she stopped me in my tracks when she told me, "I did it for *you*, Mom! Because you're always busy doing everything and I wanted you to have a break."

Guys. *They see us.*

I know, I know...being a parent is a thankless job most days. We work, we *never stop cooking*, we clean the endless tornado that is our children, we run errands, we schedule every activity, we plan every event, and all we ask for in return is a few minutes to ourselves...which we don't often get. And we feel like no one sees or appreciates us for nearly killing ourselves doing it all. But they do.

Whatever you're doing as a parent? It's enough. Stop beating yourself up for not doing more.

Because those children you're working so hard for? You're more than enough in their eyes. You're everything to them. And isn't that all that *really* matters at the end of the day?

YEAR 5 | DAY 111

When we moved into this house four years ago, I wiped the kitchen counters down meticulously, almost obsessively, all day long. While I loved the color and finish of the countertops, they showed *everything* - water rings from every glass that rested there, every crumb that managed to escape a plate, even perfect handprints from our toddler.

And for a while, I wished that no one would sit there. Sit at the kitchen table, I urged visitors in my mind, whose weathered finish covered a multitude of sins. And yet, the kitchen island was and continues to act as the main gathering place for guests in our home.

As children run around our home, the adults convene around the island to visit over coffee. As I put the finishing touches on meals and lay out plates and silverware for small gatherings, family and friends join me at the island to chat and offer their help. And as I throw together sandwiches for lunch or cook family dinners at night, my five-year-old sits at the island with her toys or crayons and chats with me as I cook.

And as time passed I realized…that's a good thing!

Those water rings and crumbs? They're signs that we're breaking bread with others.

The perfect handprints that instantly reappear 30 seconds after I wipe them away? They're evidence that our home is full of *life*. And it's life that's comfortable and sometimes messy, but full of love.

This island is a gathering place. And gathering places are going to get dirty.

Sure, I'll wipe down the island at the end of the day after putting my daughter to bed. And I'll enjoy those few blissful hours of spotless, sparkling countertops.

But until then, I'll allow these signs of life to stay for a while. I'll allow my daughter to feel free to visit with her momma and sketch her ideas and live her life without the paranoia that comes with maintaining a picture perfect home. Because isn't that what home is all about in the first place?

YEAR 5 | DAY 114

One of the bonuses of parenting small children is that you get to experience the warmth and connection of putting your child to bed roughly three to five times every single night! ...Please send help.

YEAR 5 | DAY 117

Step 1: Load up a charcuterie board with all of the foods you need to clear out of your fridge.

Step 2: Tell your kid it's a special picnic lunch.

Step 3: Watch them enthusiastically eat/clear out your fridge for you.

Step 4: Mic drop.

YEAR 5 | DAY 118

Dear stranger at the skate park,

Today my five-year-old bit it *hard* coming down a ramp. The last time she fell, I ran to her side and seemed to sap her strength with my arrival so this time, I stood at a distance.

When her coach asked her if she was okay, she choked out a "No!" through tears. And then you, stranger? You jumped in from 50 feet away without missing a beat.

"Get iiiiit! Did you see her jump right back up?! Dang, she's crazy!!" You clapped your hands and yelled loud enough to reach her heart right where it had landed in the pit of her stomach, and drag it back up to her chest again.

She smiled...a *huge* smile. Because you didn't know it, but she's always dreamed of people cheering for her at the skatepark. And there you were, cheering.

She walked over to the bench where I stood, chugged water like Napoleon Dynamite, and marched her board back up to the ramp to try again.

Stranger, your 13 words brought my daughter's dream to life, bumped her courage and grit up 10 levels, and brought *so* much comfort and encouragement to this mother's heart.

Ya'll...this world is full of good people. Be one of them. You never know the impact that a few words, just a few *seconds* of your time, could make on someone's day and life.

ADJUSTING

YEAR 5 | DAY 122

Well folks, I said it earlier this week and I'll say it again...*this world is full of good people!*

I made a miscalculation this afternoon that left me with a 26" adult bike facing a Volkswagen Jetta and it wasn't looking good for me. See, I was planning to haul a disassembled bike in my trunk, then put it together at home. So imagine my surprise when they rolled it out fully assembled and ready to go!

It was just me, my daughter, and a bike jammed halfway into the backseat, all struggling together in the parking lot, when I heard a voice behind me. "Need some help?"

Guys...this sweet older couple who were clearly making a quick stop for just a few things could have easily kept walking to their car. I wouldn't have even noticed them walk by, I was so caught up trying to tetris this thing into my car.

But no...they stopped and helped me wheel the bike into my backseat, while cautioning roughly 100 times, "Be careful for the baby!" (my daughter) When it wasn't looking hopeful and I assured them I didn't want to further burden them and would just have to come back with a bigger car, *they ran to their car for a toolbox*, took off the front wheel, and managed to fit the bike in the rest of the way (with the window down).

Who does that?! Good people, that's who.

169

Because of their selfless assist, I rode a bike this afternoon for the first time in 15 years with my daughter riding beside me, yelling, "Steady! Steaaaaady!" To say she was thrilled to ride bikes with her mom would be an understatement.

Social media and politicians and news stations would like us to focus our full attention on all of the bad things happening in the world. And if you listen to them alone, you'll believe this world is a sad and hopeless place.

But it's not.

Look out, friend! Look up. There are good people all around you. There are smiling faces, there are conversations with strangers in grocery store lines, there are small and big acts of selfless service all around us...if you're looking for them.

Say what you will, but I believe the world is still a very good place...especially San Antonio.

YEAR 5 | DAY 135

As it turns out, my
child is now
officially
I-know-we-just-
bought-that-last-
month-but-it-
doesn't-fit-anymore
years old.

YEAR 5 | DAY 141

Her: Where did my fortune cookie fortune go?!

Me (knowing full well I threw it away two weeks ago): I'm not sure! This is why you should keep things picked up – so you can always find what you're looking for!

I'm now my mother.

ADJUSTING

YEAR 5 | DAY 144

Have you ever taken a "before" photo? You know, those pics where you pose to show how far your stomach puffs out or the exact amount of jiggle in your legs before embarking on a "30-day challenge" or "3-day reset" or whatever other name caught your eye and motivated you to pursue better health?

I was surfing old pictures last night when I came across a "before" photo I took several years ago. There I was striking that familiar pose, my face fully focused on capturing down to the tiniest detail of my state of health.

But right next to it, I noticed another picture. My daughter and I were attending her weekly music class when she had decided to plaster her face with stickers and make silly faces for the camera with her momma.

And I realized that even though I had just been standing in the mirror the day before, criticizing those extra 30 pounds...the thought had never even crossed my daughter's mind. And even if someone had pointed it out to her, she wouldn't have cared one bit.

She cared that her mom was sitting right next to her, "criss-cross applesauce," in her music class. She cared that her mom trekked downtown with her every month to watch the local children's theater over M&Ms and talk about her favorite parts the entire drive home. She cared that her mom paused whatever she was doing to sit next to her while she ate her peanut butter and jelly sandwich at the kitchen island.

Yes, it's important that we take care of ourselves, that we eat healthy foods and move our bodies and for crying out loud, swap in a water for at least one of our iced coffees. But we have to be careful that we don't miss what's *most* important – our motivation for having better health in the first place – these moments with our family and friends.

Because the laughs, the hugs, the late-night conversations and inside jokes and shared experiences and even the tears? Those are the moments that make life worth living...that make better health worth pursuing. And those moments don't care one tiny bit what the scale says.

So take your "before" picture, momma. But then get right back in front of the camera to make that silly face.

YEAR 5 | DAY 149

Confession time! I am a *terrible* southern wife.

I'm not southern. I was born and raised in Iowa. But now I live in the south, where I often feel like every other woman cooks huge family meals of steaks and homemade mashed potatoes, knows how to curl these big, gorgeous waves into her hair, and perfectly accessorizes every outfit with some sort of hoop earring or cute heels. And I don't know how to do any of those things.

I don't like to spend more time in the kitchen than I have to. Most meals I "cook" include a bag of microwave steamable veggies alongside a bag of 90-second microwave rice.

My hair has exactly two styles – straightened or ponytail. And I'm not talking those super cute ponytails with lots of body and wave...I'm talking a gym pony, flat to my head, looking like I'm about to go for a jog.

I tend to wear the same few things over and over. I know what I like and what's comfortable and I sometimes wear those things more often than is probably socially acceptable.

And those things used to really bother me. They're things that can make you stick out in a sea of perfectly-styled hair and outfits. They come out when you invite people over for the third time and realize you've already used up your two good recipes on their last visits.

But these last few years, I've realized it's not only okay if I don't always fit in, but it would be a disservice to myself and to God if I tried to force myself into that image. Because God made me the way that I am on purpose. He was very deliberate in ironing out the details of my personality and gifts and even appearance.

I may not be an incredible cook, hosting big family brunches full of biscuits and gravy. But I'm incredible at listening to my family and friends pour out their hearts, and feel God has given me the gift of relating to and encouraging others.

I may drop my daughter off to school in gym shorts and a ponytail, with absolutely zero intentions of going to the gym. But I'm sure as heck approachable! While I enjoy dressing up and accessorizing occasionally, I don't care if I look like I don't have my stuff together most days... because I don't.

God didn't give me the gift of cooking or entertaining like Martha Stewart. He didn't make me naturally gifted at creating Pinterest-worthy projects or heck, even following written directions.

Those are all *amazing* gifts that can be used for His kingdom! I just don't have them.

But God *did* make me honest and *very*, very bad at hiding my true feelings...which has resulted in a million different heart-to-heart conversations with friends and strangers. God gave me next-level patience, a long-term mindset, and the exact words I need to communicate clearly and concisely.

As of right now, I think he made me this way so that I could connect with and encourage others and both survive and balance out my child's creative and eccentric personality.

As for the future? Who knows where or how God may use those gifts! But the fact is that he can't use or further develop them if I'm too busy longing for others' gifts.

It's time we stop wishing we had what others have and embrace all of the treasures that God has placed in each of us. Because when we begin to seek out and honor our own God-given personality and gifts, He can begin to show us exactly how He's always intended us to live.

YEAR 5 | DAY 163

Made the mistake of asking my five-year-old what we should get our dog for his birthday. Twenty minutes later, I'm still explaining why we won't be buying Petey a nightcap, but yes, of course he would look so handsome in one.

YEAR 5 | DAY 172

Before I could deposit it directly in the trash, my daughter spotted the Amazon toy catalog in our pile of mail and begged to have it. She then spent *hours* circling *and* drawing arrows to all of the things she wanted. She cut out the pages with circles, stapled them all back together in a different order, then "read" it to me like it was a *New York Times* bestseller.

And as a parent, her passion to own each of the circled toys hurt my heart a little. Because what parent doesn't want to shower their child with gifts, especially when they show such enthusiasm toward each one? I'd love to buy her every single thing she desires.

But (a) I'm not rich and (b) I know I'd be doing her a disservice. And in a lot of ways, it's helping me to understand God and why He doesn't always give us the things we want.

Because she circled some things simply because her friends have it. And that fact is the beginning and end of her desire because if she's honest with herself, *she* doesn't actually have a genuine interest in it.

She circled some things because they looked flashy or exciting. But she has no idea what they are or how they work. And I know she'll never actually play with that toy after the excitement of receiving it has fizzled out....because I know her.

Some of the things she circled would hurt or delay her growth and development. What she needs most at this age is time outside developing motor skills and time with friends and family developing social skills. I love her too much to give her toys or games that would hinder that development.

Some of the things she circled are waaaaay beyond her maturity or understanding. She's not ready for them, but I'll consider them when she is.

Some toys she already has a version of in her room, but she doesn't play with or appreciate it. Why would I give her more of that thing?

And frankly, buying her *all* of the things she ever wants will make it much harder to avoid her becoming a spoiled and entitled adult, which wouldn't do either of us any favors.

All of that to say...maybe God isn't giving you the thing you most want because He loves you too much to do that. Maybe He sees the big picture when you don't and can't. Maybe what feels like an unanswered prayer is one of God's greatest gifts to you.

Maybe.

I guess he likes big butts and he cannot lie about that! 'Cause it's just true!

- my child's deep
  thoughts on
  Sir Mix-a-Lot

YEAR 5 | DAY 177

Me to my mom: I'm 35 years old, I've gotta call the shots for my own family.

Also me to my mom: Look at this comparison chart and tell me which health insurance plan I should choose.

Hey! No ribbon dancing until you brush your teeth!

- things I say now

YEAR 5 | DAY 195

Sometimes motherhood is grabbing a slice of cold pizza from the fridge to eat on the bathroom floor while your five-year-old takes a bath...because there's not enough time in the day and you just realized it's 1:00 and you haven't eaten anything yet. It's your child asking to share a bite, even though she swears she doesn't like pepperoni and you promised her a sandwich after her bath.

Sometimes motherhood is finding yourself sharing cold pizza with your child in the bathtub while you sit on a toilet seat, chatting about her plans for the day and answering her questions about your own childhood. And it's realizing that bathtub pizza moments can be just as special as kitchen table homemade meal moments...that it was never about the meal or the setting, but about the company.

ADJUSTING

YEAR 5 | DAY 206

Daughter to her new Lego minifigures on the way home from the store: You're coming to live with us now. Mom only has three rules!

Me: (turning down the radio because I'm curious to know what three rules cover everything)

Daughter:
1. You get what you get and you don't throw a fit.
2. Don't disobey mom.
3. Don't run away at night to live in the jungle.

Yep. Those are all actual rules I've had to set. And yeah...that about covers it.

YEAR 5 | DAY 214

This morning, my daughter declared, "Let me find my victory dance socks. Today is gonna be the best day of my life!" I don't know what makes those particular socks victory dance socks, but I pray your day starts with the same hope and positivity!

ADJUSTING

YEAR 5 | DAY 220

Me, casually at 7:00 PM: Maybe we can ride bikes tomorrow...

My child at my bedside at 5:30 AM the next day: Why are you still sleeping? I thought you said we were riding bikes this morning!

YEAR 5 | DAY 222

Me: What should we get Dad for Christmas?

Her: I was thinking of putting a swimming pool in the backyard.

Me: …

Her: We should probably start digging now.

Me: …I was thinking something from Amazon.

Her: Oh.

ADJUSTING

YEAR 5 | DAY 226

Me: You need a bath tonight.

Her: I just had one a few days ago!!

Me: Yeah, that's how they work...you have to keep taking them.

Her: Ugh, it's like you're obsessed with being clean! That's not what's most important in life, you know?

YEAR 5 | DAY 230

Try using your hot breath to warm up your kid's deodorant on a cold morning...and slip so your lip grazes the deodorant *just one time*...and your kid will tell everyone she sees, *everyone*, that her mom licked her deodorant.

YEAR 5 | DAY 232

Once or twice a week, after I drop my daughter off at school, I walk a four-mile loop around the school's neighborhood. I call family or friends, listen to audiobooks, or just think along my walk. It's my little sliver of me time.

And every walk for the last month, I've crossed paths with the same penny. It sits at the edge of a church parking lot and despite traffic and recent rains, has somehow managed to remain in the exact same spot.

And today it struck me that life is happening all around this penny. People are constantly stepping over it to attend christenings, weddings, and funerals held inside the church. Loads more walk past it as they circle the same loop I do, exercising with friends or spouses, reining in dogs on leashes, or gliding jogging strollers across the parking lot. But despite the world continuing to spin around it, the penny doesn't move.

You don't have to move. Not one inch. You can keep sitting in the same circumstances that are draining and depressing you. You can avoid confronting that issue that's been hanging over your head for years because it's easier to ignore it.

But is that what you want? To sit exactly where you are, in the same circumstances you've always been, while life keeps moving forward all around you?

Friend, you only get one life to live. *Do that thing you've been meaning to do*. Reconcile that relationship...or end it!

Whichever needs to be done. Put yourself out there, take that leap at work, learn that thing you've always wanted to learn.

Life is about learning and growing...and moving forward. It's about having the courage to fall down 100 times and the determination to get back up 101. But if you want to move, you have to move. (Ingenious quote, I know.)

So here's your sign to do that thing. Now go. Change your life. Change the world.

ADJUSTING

YEAR 5 | DAY 240

I just finished creating the weirdest playlist of my life. Despite it requiring me to google stupid things like "song at the end of *Chipmunks Road Chip*," I'm especially proud of this Christmas gift for my daughter.

I won a 4th generation iPod Touch at work *nine years* ago, jogged with it on a near-daily basis for about five years, then sentenced it to life in a drawer a few years ago in favor of listening to music on my phone.

I've spent the last week deleting my old music from it, removing all but a few apps, and then collecting the random songs she currently loves, including "Bamboleo," "Johnny B. Goode," the *Home Alone* soundtrack, and the song at the end of *Napoleon Dynamite*. I promise you this will be one of her favorites, if not her favorite gift this year.

All that to say that you don't have to spend hundreds of dollars to give your kids a great Christmas. I believe most kids more so want to know you're listening...and that what's important to them is important to you. And those things are free.

YEAR 5 | DAY 242

Ever wish you could try your hand at brushing and blow drying someone's hair while they twirl and dance and rap about squirrels? Become a parent! All your wildest dreams will come true!!

YEAR 5 | DAY 243

Beneath our Christmas tree this year, you'll find four presents addressed to...stuffed animals. It all started at the dollar store, where my daughter was picking out small presents for friends and gasped dramatically when she caught sight of a tiny Etch-a-Sketch. "Cheetah (her favorite stuffy) would *love* that!"

But then she saw a monster truck...and figured Honey might be jealous if Cheetah received a present and he didn't. And what about Polar Bear? And Beary?!

1. Annoying
2. More money
3. More time spent at the dollar store when we were juuuuust about to leave with our sanity

But I figured, who am I – for the sake of 10 more minutes and 5 more bucks – to kill the compassion and enthusiasm of a generous young heart? Who am I to teach her that we don't have time to think of others? Or that it's too much of a pain?

I mean, it *is* a pain. But it's a pain worth enduring today for a brighter and kinder future...for humans and stuffies alike.

I can't wait to see Cheetah's reaction to his Etch-a-Sketch.

YEAR 5 | DAY 244

Just learned my daughter decided that kindergarten was still lots of fun, even though it turned out it wasn't about gardening after all. I never thought to explain the name...

ADJUSTING

YEAR 5 | DAY 255

I'd love for my work from home desk in my bedroom to look sleek and clean and magazine-worthy, but unfortunately my favorite flowers don't readily flow with any HGTV designs. See, every time my daughter finds a flower in her huge Lego bin, she shouts in excitement and hurries to my desk to add it to my Lego stem bouquet, proudly proclaiming, "I found this for you, Mom!"

And I wouldn't trade a single Lego flower for its more aesthetically-appealing alternative. These flowers, this home, has been fashioned by love. It might not be trendy but darn it, it's beautiful.

YEAR 5 | DAY 257

My mom doesn't do everything exactly the way I do. She feeds my daughter different foods, offers different drinks. They do different things together than we do at home.

Sure, sometimes it seems excessive. I mean, does my daughter really need McDonald's *and* cookies *and* marshmallows toasted over their backyard campfire, all within 24 hours?

But here's the thing – it's only for a few days...or sometimes just a few hours. Maybe my daughter will come home wired. That's definitely a possibility. Maybe it will take a day or two to get her back into our home routine.

But she will *also* come home loved, happy, and full of new memories shared with her grandparents – memories she'll treasure one day if/when my mother's dream of being swept up in a tornado comes true.

But seriously...my mother won't always be with us. And when she leaves one day, those memories will be all my daughter has.

So please...show grandparents some grace, if not for their sake, for your child's sake. Your child might be thrown off their routine for a short time, but will gain adaptability, treasured memories, and even more love than you alone can provide them. And who doesn't need that?

ADJUSTING

YEAR 5 | DAY 265

Putting my daughter to bed tonight:

Me: Okay, I love you! Lay down.

Her: Hey, mom?

Me: Yes? Lay down.

Her: You know that song, "Hey, I just met you...and this is crazy?"

Me: Yep. Lay down.

Her: Why is it crazy?

Me: Because she just met him and already wants to be friends. Lay down.

Her: Why's she say, "Call me *maybe*? Why maybe?"

Me: Siiiiigh...because she doesn't want to sound too crazy, so she's like...maybe?? Lay down.

Her: What number is she giving him? Her number, how old she is?!

Me: Her phone number. *Please* lay down so I can pee. I'm begging you. Lay down.

Her: Peeing's not what's most important, Mom. Family is most important.

Me: (dying in a heap of exhaustion on the floor)

ADJUSTING

YEAR 5 | DAY 272

I'm still working from home in my bedroom and have been since last March. My daughter, in an attempt to sneak in and see me whenever she can, always insists on using my bathroom whenever I'm in my "office."

Yesterday I asked her to please close the doors behind her. She asked why I wanted the doors closed and rather than tell her it's to make sure no murderers emerge from the open doors behind me, I told her it made me uncomfortable, like *someone* might walk through.

Five-year-old: Like a monster?

Me (laughing): Maybe!

Five-year-old (laughing): There *are* no monsters! Anyways, if you keep thinking about something too much, sometimes your brain tricks you and makes you believe it's true. But it's not. You just have to change the channel, Mom!

She was repeating back to me what I had told her just a few nights prior when she was too afraid of gremlins (don't ask) to fall asleep. But I just couldn't stop thinking about what she said. Because it expands beyond so much more than scary shadows.

Our thoughts are very powerful. And if we sit with a negative, untrue thought for too long ("I'm not good enough," "I'm a failure," "My family would be better off without me," etc.), it *feels* like reality, doesn't it?

But it's not. It's just a thought that you sat with for too long and therefore, made more powerful.

Change the channel, friend. I tell my daughter to change the channel when gremlins are playing out in her head and I can change the channel when I call myself names or doubt my worth. I can even change the channel when I'm sitting in anger, bitterness, or unforgiveness. And so can you.

Those thoughts aren't true and they certainly aren't serving you well. So stop binge watching them and see what else is on.

ADJUSTING

YEAR 5 | DAY 285

Me: It's time for your bath.

Her: How about first thing tomorrow?

Me: Today.

Her: What about after I ride my bike?

Me: Nope. Now.

Her: What about a lick bath, so it's less wet?

Me: A *lick* bath?

Her: Yeah, like lion moms give their cubs.

Me: ......I'm not a lion. So...no.

Her: Siiiiigh, you *always* want to do things your way, don't you?

YEAR 5 | DAY 286

I'm pretty sure that if dishwasher Tetris was a sport, I would be an Olympian.

Are the dishes stacked so close together they might not get as clean? Possibly.

Is there a chance the top rack will break off under the weight I've packed on it? Absolutely.

But the most important thing to remember is that I'm a champion.

YEAR 5 | DAY 287

...and this is why we don't blow whistles while we're eating yogurt!

- things I say now

YEAR 5 | DAY 293

I spent my lunch break today at the neighborhood park with my daughter. She asked for help climbing into the "spinny seat" as she calls it, then held onto my arm with a death grip while yelling, "Spin me, Momma!"

"How can I spin you if you don't let go of my arm?" I asked.

But she tried anyway, first holding my hand above her head and twisting it until I thought she might pull my skin clean off, then trading hands back and forth, neither technique really doing the trick.

"If you want a real spin, you'll have to let go," I told her. "You don't have to spin fast if you don't want to. This might just be your new favorite thing! But you'll never find out if you don't let go of my hand."

And it made me think of myself, holding onto what's comfortable because…well, it's comfortable. It's known.

There have been new opportunities, new ideas, cropping up recently that I'm not sure I've given fair consideration, all because I prefer comfortable things… familiar things. Don't we all?

How many of us are sitting in places where sure, we may be competent and yes, we know what to expect, but maybe we're not happy or fulfilled? If there was ever a good time to try something new, it's now. And if there was ever a good year to let go of comfortable things that are no longer serving you, it's this year!

206

Because that thing you've been meaning to try? It might just be your new favorite thing!

YEAR 5 | DAY 296

Our dog is now an old man – 91 in dog years! And as might be expected, he's getting a little grumpier, a little slower, a little more annoying at times.

He might snap a bit if you touch him before he sees you. After all, he's lost a lot of his hearing and is, understandably, easily startled. He needs to go out more often and walks at a maddeningly slow pace to the back door.

And did I mention he follows me everywhere? I'm constantly tripping over him and carefully sliding him out of my way.

But somehow, I find loads of patience for him. I remember when I met him at a shelter almost twelve years ago. I remember how he has patiently worn countless costumes and played a wide variety of roles for my daughter over the past five years. I remember the jogs together, the cuddles, the laughter at his crazy antics.

And I excuse his behavior today. Because he really is such a good boy.

But it makes me wonder if I do the same for my human family and friends. We share history together too! We've shared experiences and cuddles and laughter.

But when they're short with me, I'm so good at focusing on all of their worst qualities. I remember the last 10 times they acted rudely toward me rather than the last 100 times we laughed together. I focus on their 5 bad traits instead of their 50 good ones.

Granted, humans have more control over their words and actions. They're not at the mercy of their instincts.

But they still have instincts. They still have frustrations and disappointments and bad days that can make them snap at others sometimes.

So today, I'm trying to be more understanding. Because if a dog deserves a little grace sometimes, how much more do our loved ones?

I'm so thankful my
5-year-old bought a
dollar store flute
just hours before our
days-long power
outage.

One of my favorite things to do is wander around my house playing a rousing game of where-the-heck-did-I-leave-my-coffee.

CHAPTER 5 | TRUSTING

YEAR 5 | DAY 306

I just finished putting my five-year-old to bed. After we say our good nights, I often wander around the house collecting the odds and ends that escaped our bedtime cleaning sweep. And tonight, I stumbled upon her drawing of four cats.

As I inspected and compared the cats, I realized she drew them four different ways, with different ears and head shapes, different paws and poses. But if you looked at any of the cats individually, they were all fantastic cats in and of themselves. And it made me think about all of the different ways we can approach parenthood.

We could be the mom who stays at home with her children and logs endless hours of quality time. We could be the working mom who only sees her children for an hour or two a day, but teaches them hard work and smashing stereotypes by her example.

We could be the mom who throws frozen pre-made pancakes in the microwave. (Me!) Or we could be the mom who makes a warm, homemade breakfast every morning without fail.

We could be the mom throwing Pinterest-worthy themed parties for our kids. Or the one ordering decorations on Amazon Prime two days before the party and praying they make it on time.

We could be the mom pursuing her dreams, working hard to turn a side gig into a career. Or the mom focused on her health journey. Or the mom who's on no particular journey, simply enjoying the company of her family and friends.

And no matter what our version of parenthood looks like, we are still fantastic parents. We may look different than other parents. We may have different strengths. But we're getting the job done.

So don't beat yourself up when you're scrolling social media, comparing yourself to others. Fantastic parents come in all shapes and sizes...including yours.

YEAR 5 | DAY 308

Me: (in the bathroom, attempting to pee)

Her (throwing open the door): Mom, I'm trying to draw Spider-Man, but need to see the details. Think you could help me pull up a picture on the iPad?

Me: Babe, give me two minutes! Close the door!

Her: (steps inside tiny bathroom, closes the door behind her)

Me: ......

Her: ......

Me: I meant close the door with you *outside* of the bathroom.

Her (sighing and leaving): Well, this is all very confusing.

TRUSTING

Agreed to play with my child and in less than five minutes, I was eaten by a shark, talked to the shark's heart while in his stomach, was eaten by his *heart* (?!), met rock-and-roll Jesus (because Jesus lives in your heart), who played me a guitar riff, and this is why I'm tired.

YEAR 5 | DAY 333

My daughter wanted to play basketball last weekend. Should be fun, right? No.

Because she believes she should be able to dribble, shoot, and do all kinds of tricks. But her greatest *actual* basketball achievement to date is hitting the net with the ball...a fact that quickly frustrates her.

To say I wasn't super excited would be an understatement. *But* we packed up the ball and some water and drove to the neighborhood court anyways.

After about twenty minutes of attempting to shoot, I could tell she was reaching a mental wall. So I suggested we take a quick break at the picnic table.

And at that table, we had a completely *fantastic* time. We talked about basketball, about skateboarding, about how very hard it is to keep trying and getting back up when you fail at something over and over. We marveled together at the scooter tricks the boy next door performed for her while pretending he didn't see her there. We chatted about her upcoming birthday, about the new style she was going for with her clothes and accessories, and about the exact reasons she liked Pokémon.

And I would have missed out on all of those things if I had acted on one of the 10 million reasons I could think of to *not* play basketball that day.

Hang in there, parents! Some parts of parenting are not our favorites. In fact, as our kids grow and develop their own hobbies and interests, there's a very good chance we'll be asked to join things that make us groan internally.

But those are the places where we can best meet our kids. By taking that time and showing interest in our children's interests, we're opening a door to connect with them. And maybe just basketball games will flow through that open door. Or maybe deeper conversations and connections that last far beyond the game itself will flow through.

Open that door....even if you don't like or enjoy it....even if you'd rather be doing something else. Because your kids have so much to say and share. They just need an opening.

YEAR 5 | DAY 345

Today, I paused for me.

Today, even though I had to clean the house and do our taxes and update my book manuscript, I paused anyway. And I went to the doctor for a physical.

Today, I paused to take my blood pressure and pulse ox, to have my eyes, ears, and throat inspected, to draw blood, and to discuss my health concerns with my doctor.

And today, I learned that I'm completely normal. That sure, I've neglected myself this past year, but no more than any other human.

Today, I learned that my utter exhaustion could likely be improved with natural supplements...and that even though I had assumed nothing could be done to stop my ears from ringing after eight (very long) years, that I actually have several promising options.

No, seeing my doctor didn't magically resolve every problem. But it brought me one step closer to resolution. And it reminded me that I am worthy of the same time, attention, and care that I regularly give to others.

Today, I paused for me. And it felt fantastic. I may just make a habit of this...

YEAR 5 | DAY 351

Her: Today at school, we talked about psychics.

Me: Psychics?

Her: Life psychics! Like larva, pupa, ladybug, *egg*!

Me: Are you sure it's not life cycles?

Her: Oh, yeah. That's it! Did you know that ladybugs have four wings? Two soft and two hard?

Me: Wow! I didn't!

Her: Did you know that bees show each other where to find flowers by *dancing*?

Me: I didn't! That's really interesting!

Her: *Did you know that elephant mothers like to start fires to keep their babies warm?!*

Me: ......

Her: Science.

Me: Are you sur-

Her: *Science.*

I recently bought a photo board with zero plans for where to hang it in our home. I just knew I loved it and it was on clearance for $3.

When I asked my daughter what photos I should hang on it, she suggested a picture of her skateboarding, then said, "Oh! You can make it a board full of things I do that make you proud." She knew I was proud of her skateboarding and wanted more of her feats displayed on the wall.

I started looking through my photos for inspiration but quickly found that my favorite moments weren't of her catching a baseball or doing a bike trick or winning awards. So I printed my favorites and displayed them.

My daughter looked confused as I positioned them on the board. "You're proud of me for laying on the couch with Dad?"

"Not laying," I explained. "I'm proud that you have such a kind and loving heart, and are always helping and loving on your dad."

"And you're proud of me for playing with Cheetah (her stuffy)?!"

"I'm proud of how creative you are! When you made those matching knight costumes for you and Cheetah, I remember being so amazed that you pictured something in your head and just…made it!"

"But you're proud of me for my skateboarding tricks too?" she asked, peering at the last photo.

"Of course I am! And I'm *also* proud of how hard you worked to learn to skateboard! It took a lot of practice and I know how frustrated you felt some days, but you just kept at it. Not everyone can do that!"

She smiled and I could watch her thoughts through her eyes as she studied each photo, realizing that her parents were proud of her skills and abilities, of course, but *most* proud of her character.

I think it's important for our kids to know that we're proud of *them* as people…not just of their athletic and academic accomplishments. It's not the good grade itself we appreciate, but all of the hard work and determination it took to get there. It's not the trophy for winning state, or even the home run that won the game, but all of the moments leading up to it where our children demonstrated discipline, perseverance, and resilience.

Because they can't always receive the highest grade. And they can't win every game for the rest of their lives. But when they're confident in their own character, they can find the strength to get back up and try again. And isn't that what we all need?

YEAR 5 | DAY 354

When we bought a little dome to grow ladybugs from larvae, we said, "Bob (our fish) always seems bored. Let's put it next to him and give him something to look at!"

My daughter and I have spent the last two weeks *so* happy for Bob. "Look! He *loves* having something new to look at! Oh my gosh, I think he loves those little bugs. He's adopted them as his own babies, always watching over them!"

Today I learned that beta fish eat bugs. And it turns out we've been torturing Bob for weeks now.

TRUSTING

YEAR 5 | DAY 356

Confession: Whenever our schedules allow, on the very few and far between days we don't have to set alarm clocks, I let my daughter watch too much TV. She wakes up, snags the cup of chocolate milk I leave for her in the fridge, nestles into my bed beside me, and watches a baaaaarely audible movie while I attempt to sleep a while longer.

Frankly, I struggle to get even five hours of sleep most nights thanks to my work/home schedules, so whatever will buy me a few more minutes of sleep is (mostly) permissible.

But for so long, I would feel bad about it. She doesn't need to start her day in front of a screen, I'd tell myself. She's been watching TV for almost two hours now, I'd lament when I'd finally roll out of bed. She should be doing things outside, engaging with others, being productive!

But recently, she told me while nestled in beside me, "I love your room, Mom!"

"Why's that?" I asked.

"It's just very calm. I like the quiet and I like cuddling with you and it's just...calm."

The look in her eye told me it was a safe space for her, an opportunity to rest and be held. While I was busy beating myself up, she was creating memories of calm and quiet mornings with her momma.

Our kids don't care about what parenting books have to say. They're not losing sleep over a little extra screen time or a dirty house or the fact that you ordered out again instead of making a home-cooked meal.

They just enjoy you. They treasure time spent with you, even if/when it's time spent doing not much of anything.

I have no idea how much TV I watched as a kid. I don't remember what we ate for dinner outside of a few family favorites. I have no clue how clean our house was or wasn't. But I have hundreds of treasured memories of spending time with my family, many of them doing nothing at all.

Don't beat yourself up over things no one else is beating you up over. Don't kill yourself to accomplish tasks and goals that may be great, but aren't right or even possible for you on this day or in this season.

Your kids enjoy *you*. That's enough. The rest is just icing.

YEAR 6 | DAY 1

Does anyone else store their one-off, random items in a certain place thinking, oh yeah, this makes perfect sense, I'll *definitely* remember that I put this here...then can't find it later to save their life? I guess what I'm really saying is, if you find a fish-scooping net, lemme know.

YEAR 6 | DAY 3

"Close your eyes. You're safe."

It was a phrase I used often several nights ago as my daughter lay beside me, struggling to sleep in the midst of heavy rains and hail. She could hear the weather report my husband was watching in the next room and kept hearing our city name and "tornado" used in the same sentence.

As she lay there fixating her eyes on the window, she flinched at every flash of lightning, shuddered at every roll of thunder. So...I told her to stop looking around.

"Close your eyes. You're safe."

It reminded me of when Jesus called Peter out to walk on the water of a stormy sea in Matthew 14. Peter jumped boldly from the boat and began walking on the water toward Jesus. But when he shifted his gaze to the waves crashing around him, he began to sink.

I *love* the Message version of what Jesus said to him: "Faint-heart, what got into you?"

See, the things we fix our eyes on? They get *into* us. They mess with our minds and our hearts. They can make us forget God's promises, His truths.

Sure, we start out boldly following after Christ and His calling, but then we see the unrest in the world around us. We see those things beyond our control. We see things that worry and frighten us, the things that are right in front of our faces and crashing down all around us and *so* very hard to ignore. And they get into us...and sink us.

Close your eyes. You're safe.

The world may be beyond your control, but it's not beyond God's.

Stop focusing on the waves. Stop dwelling on your worries.

Fix your eyes on Jesus. You're safe.

YEAR 6 | DAY 5

Our dog died last week. We had known his neurological system wasn't quite up to speed lately, but something finally broke Monday morning. After 24 hours of examining and testing and waiting and medicating and more testing and more waiting, we determined the right and best thing we could do for him was to allow him to rest after nearly 14 years of faithful love and service to our family.

It was a very hard day that made for a hard week. But through it all, I was reminded of the life-changing importance of friendships.

We received a million DMs and texts from people checking in with us and offering their condolences, loads of friends confirming what we already knew, that Petey was "such a good boy!" Then we opened the front door to find some goodies and a kind note, then to find another box, filled with a sweet photo frame that would display Petey's collar and a book for our daughter, all about "dog heaven." The next day we received a text that *more* goodies were waiting on our front porch.

And all of those texts and surprises and kind words added up to turn what was a really terrible day into a day where I felt more supported and loved than I had in years. (Thank you, friends and family!) I ended the day feeling incredibly grateful.

All of that to say this – send the text. Comment on the social media post. Better yet, call your friend to see how they're doing. You might think those things don't really matter, that your saying, "I'm sorry for your loss," or "I've been there," or "I'm praying for you" is a small and insignificant thing. But you'd be wrong.

Because whether you contribute a drop of water or a glassful, you're filling their cup. You may be one of loads of people supporting and lifting them up. Or you might be the only one, and a voice that is desperately needed.

Worst case scenario, your friend thinks you're thoughtful. Best case, you save their life with the words they most needed to hear. Those aren't bad odds for what would take less than a minute of your time!

People need people. That's just a fact. And at the end of the day, people are really all we have (*after God).

So love your people. And one day when you lose a loved one or receive a hard diagnosis or are just having a terrible, stressful day, they'll be there to love you back.

"A friend loves at all times, and a brother is born for a time of adversity" (Proverbs 17:17).

YEAR 6 | DAY 9

Husband: Aw man, I worked so hard on this gravy and it just didn't turn out.

Six-year-old: No, dad! It's really great!!

Husband: Awww! Thank you, baby!

Six-year-old: Yeah! It reminds me exactly of the mud pies I make at school.

Husband: .....thanks.

YEAR 6 | DAY 10

Before I became a mother, I had so many plans, all of which I knew, just *knew* would work.

I would follow a regular schedule. I would make sure that my child reached all of her milestones early. I would read countless books to my baby, then personally teach her to read and write and equip her to make straight A's and graduate with honors and become a brain surgeon. I would do everything right. But then I actually *became* a mother...and also a train wreck...all on the same day.

Motherhood is hard...and messy...and nothing goes the way you planned or expected it to go. Ever.

Motherhood is exhausting and thankless and selfless... and transformative. It tears down everything you thought you knew and puts the pieces back together in a way that's so very far from perfect and yet...better.

My daughter has made me more adaptable, more resilient, more patient, more empathetic, more curious, more creative, and stronger than I could have ever been without her. She's forced me into a position where I've had no choice but to rethink the way I do everything, reassess what's actually important, and redistribute my time and energy accordingly.

She's pushed me into a role where I can't be perfect. Perfection is out of the question. But it's a role where I can be honest...and open...and humble.

Motherhood has given me a front row seat to life, seeing a baby grow into the person they'll become, marveling at how their mind works, how their heart loves, how their soul somehow connects with yours in such a way that you feel they never really left your body since you carried them in your womb.

Motherhood will break you over and over again. But then it will lift you and carry you to places you would have never been otherwise, places you never knew you wanted to go.

Happy Mother's Day, to all those who are mothers by blood or by choice or in spirit. You may feel some days like you're being buried alive. But the truth is that you're being planted to grow into something brand new. You'll see.

YEAR 6 | DAY 17

Ever wish you were urged to inspect, marvel at, and verbally acknowledge each individual flake of a bowl of Frosted Flakes? If so, you would really, *really* love being a parent. Really.

YEAR 6 | DAY 19

Me (serving a pasta dish my daughter and I had just cooked together): You made this! Can you believe it?! Sometimes people name their special recipes or dishes. What do you think we should name this dish?

Six-year-old: (long, very contemplative pause)...... mmmmmmmmmm......Timmy.

YEAR 6 | DAY 22

Here lies Debra Preston.

Death by: Hearing the same *Alvin and the Chipmunks* song over and over again until she collapsed.

Song to be played at her funeral.

Fact: Kids move slowest when it's pouring rain and you're trying to get them in the car.

YEAR 6 | DAY 34

I enjoy sharing thoughts and photos with friends on social media. I believe it can be a tool to bring us together and make us stronger for it.

But...I also think taking a million pictures of the same moment to get just the right angle, lighting, filter, and caption, can take away from the moment itself. I believe it's easy enough to capture what looks like a Hallmark moment without actually being a fully-present *part* of that moment.

I think there's something sacred about exercising privacy at times, that there's something special about a moment *just* shared with your family...no photos, no live streaming, just giving your spouse, your children, your friends 100% of your attention for the entire evening. Nope, sometimes it's not quality over quantity. Sometimes...a *lot* of times...your loved ones just want your whole heart for the whole night.

Friend, don't allow the allure of social media views and likes and comments to steal from your here and now. Don't watch every moment of your child's life from behind your phone while you snap pics and take videos. The opportunity to watch them grow and laugh and cry and *live* with your own eyes, to experience it for yourself, is a deeply sacred gift not granted to everyone.

Sure, take your picture! Take a video! Capture the moment so you can share it with grandparents and relive it later.

But then set down your phone and just breathe it in. Lock eyes with your loved ones...or that perfect sunset...or that gorgeous ceremony...and just...be there. This is living, friend. Don't miss out.

TRUSTING

YEAR 6 | DAY 36

Warning: This may be the dumbest thing I've ever written but it's true, so I'm sharing it. Please skip past my late-night thoughts if you're not in the mood.

Buccee is my daughter's kindergarten class rabbit that we offered to watch for the summer. And Buccee knows what he wants...namely, to court my husband. He knows exactly where my husband is at all times and runs at him with reckless abandon the second we open his crate. He circles and nips at my husband's feet (apparently how rabbits express their love interest) *ceaselessly*.

But what I've noticed is that Buccee knows what he wants and nothing can stop him. *Nothing.*

My husband will scoot him away from his ankles 100 times, but Buccee will return 101 times. He won't take the rejection personally. In fact, he doesn't even seem to realize (or care) that my husband isn't interested in his advances. He's blinded by passion for his dream. And hormones. But mostly, I like to think...passion.

Even after being rejected, he returns, returns, returns a million times. Sometimes he pauses to rethink his approach. He'll jump on the couch, launch off my husband's lap, and dive for his ankles again. He'll even settle for a few minutes, attempt to distract my husband with some calm pets, then go in for the kill again.

It's all coinciding with a book I'm reading that talks about how easily we allow others to shut down our dreams. They're not interested in our dreams, they don't believe in us, so they tell us no. And we take that no as our sign to stop trying.

This is the one and only time I will encourage you to be like a hormonal rabbit, I swear to you. But...keep at it, friend! Don't take rejection personally. Rejection shouldn't be your sign to stop chasing after your dream. Rejection should be your sign to rethink the way you're approaching it, to try something different.

Or heck...maybe it's your sign to just keep at it! I launched my blog over four years ago. I have not experienced wild and immediate success. But I've grown slowly and steadily.

Some weeks, I've knocked out loads of work and experienced huge wins. Some weeks, I've only managed to find 5-10 minutes to work on it at all. But I keep at it. I come back again and again and again and again. Because writing is my dream. And no one in this entire world – not internet trolls or tanking social media algorithms or rejected book proposals – can say no to my dreams except *me*.

Be like Buccee. Don't give up. Don't take it personally. Just keep at it. Rethink your approach and do it again. And again. And eat more spinach.

Good night!

TRUSTING

YEAR 6 | DAY 41

Today we visited a snake farm/zoo. It had loads of snakes (as you might have suspected) but also other wildlife, animal shows, a "mining experience," and a petting zoo.

I committed to doing one fun activity with my daughter every week this summer, since the majority of the rest of her week is spent entertaining herself at home. And since this was the week's activity, I wanted to check *every* experience there off our list.

The problem was, she didn't want to visit the petting zoo...which was a good chunk of the experience! We had already bought the animal feed, I had carried it around as we looked at lions and hyenas, and now it was time to feed animals and she was afraid.

I tried the ol' "just do it" and rushed in the gate assuming she'd follow and warm up to it and have the time of her life and thank me afterwards for pushing her out of her comfort zone. Except she didn't follow me. She ran in the opposite direction, stopped only by a free-roaming chicken who looked "a-spicious" blocking her path.

I urged her to try. "You're missing out on all the fun!" I insisted.

But instead, we settled for momma feeding goats through the fence (rather than walking inside the pen) and yelling "ew! ew! ewwwww!" as goats licked my hands and she laughed hysterically. We settled for her instructing me which baby goat to feed to ensure all were included. And it was *still great*...maybe even better.

As you're launching out into summer plans, it's okay if your kids don't participate in *everything*. Even if you think it would be fun. Even if every other kid but yours seems to love it.

Sure, sometimes they need a little push to try something new. I've done my fair share of healthy pushing. But sometimes they need a parent who will respect their insistent "no" and find a way to adapt so that they can enjoy the experience at their own pace.

It's okay if they're too afraid to swim with the dolphins....or too overwhelmed by the big crowds at that carnival...or don't like the way that goat is looking at them.

The most important part of your summer plans, and really *any* plan, is the time you spend together. If you're already there together, boom! You did it! Pat yourself on the back, rest assured your child knows you hear them, you're listening, and save yourself from some unnecessary goat slobber.

Happy summer!

YEAR 6 | DAY 51

My six-year-old told me she "had" to stop singing a song because her singing was *too* beautiful and about to make her cry and that's the kind of confidence I need in my life.

YEAR 6 | DAY 53

Me: What do you want to watch?

Her: *Grain*!

Me: *Grain*?

Her: It's a movie about a farmer who grows grain and the farm animals go on an adventure to the city...

Me: (starting to type "grain" in the search bar)

Her: ...and then the animals turn into humans because they stayed in the city for too long.

Me: ......

Her: ......

Me: ...Is this a real movie? Or a movie in your head?

Her: ......

Me: ......

Her: I'm sure *someone* made it because it sounds *awesome*, right?! Let's just google and see!

YEAR 6 | DAY 58

Last night, about 15 minutes after tucking my daughter into bed, I heard her voice calling from her bedroom down the hall. "Mom?"

"Yes?" I yelled back, hoping to avoid getting up from the recliner I had just settled into.

"Oh, it was just a test," she explained, a bit sheepishly. "I just wanted to make sure you were there."

I've been thinking about her words ever since. Because how often are our kids "testing" to make sure we're there?

Sometimes it looks like them sharing a piece of their day with us. What they're really asking is if we're available to listen.

Sometimes it's more subtle. Sometimes it's asking us to sit by them at the kitchen island while they eat their snack...or asking for help to do something we *know* they can do themselves.

Sometimes it's annoying. Sometimes I would rather sit on the couch than on that kitchen barstool. It's more comfortable, after all.

And sometimes I want to tell my daughter that she's six and she can brush her teeth on her own tonight, just like she does every other night. She doesn't need company in the bathroom.

But these are their touchpoints. These are their tests, just checking in to make sure we're still there if they need help getting their pajamas on or feel lonely eating their snack. And I'm choosing to take just a moment to say yes, I'm here.

Not because I let my child call the shots. Not even because I think she sincerely needs help changing into her pajamas that night. She doesn't.

I do it because I want her to know from first-hand experience that I'm here for her, for things big and small. I want her to so consistently hear my "yes, I'm here" that she knows it intuitively, doesn't question it for even one second.

These are the tests that are easy enough to pass but are teaching our children that we're here, we're listening, we would drop anything if they needed us to help them change into their pajamas one night...or mend their broken heart after a breakup...or care for their newborn while they catch some desperately-needed sleep.

These are our opportunities to express a deep and enduring love just by being present. And I'm here for that.

TRUSTING

My mom and stepdad live in Galveston, just a five-hour drive away. But between a pandemic, health issues, and the fact that they drive to visit us (and other nearby family) every month or two, I hadn't made the drive there in over two years.

So imagine my disappointment as we drove to visit them last weekend...after weeks of planning and packing, requesting time off work, and killing myself to knock out projects and meetings all before leaving...in the pouring rain. Imagine my internal groan looking at the weekend forecast to find a 100% chance of rain every day we'd be there. We didn't have the flexibility to change dates, so we just...drove there in the rain.

Yet right as we arrived, when we had originally planned to take the boat out for a little fishing...the rain cleared. We thanked God for the small break in weather and in fact, it made the boat ride more enjoyable with some cloud covering and cooler temperatures.

Later that evening, it cleared again and allowed for an enjoyable time on the beach. No sweating to death or worrying about dehydration. No drowning my extra white child, who somehow managed to dodge even a *tiny* gene of my family's Mexican heritage, with sunscreen.

The next morning, we were able to enjoy an hour of digging holes and building sandcastles on the beach before the rain started. We ran into and out of local restaurants, tourist stops, and candy shops, all in the rain. My daughter informed the sky through the sunroof of my mom's Jetta that fine, it could rain for a few hours, but would need to stop that evening.

And it did! She splashed in the ocean with her grandpa for *two hours*, threw oyster crackers to seagulls, and threw oyster crackers at *me*, making seagulls chase me down the beach while she laughed hysterically until she choked. And it had me thinking...our vacation was better for the rain.

When I say my daughter is extra white, I mean that even *with* sunscreen, she starts to burn within 20 minutes of being outside. Heck, she once sunburned just sitting near an open window! Within an hour of being outside, she's feeling sick from the heat and developing a rash on her face.

But this weekend, she was able to run and play for hours without a care in the world. She screamed with delight every time a wave knocked her down, investigated under the water with her goggles and reported back, and dug impressive holes in the sand with the goal of "reaching the bottom of the beach," all without the cares of the sun or heat...and all without being cold either.

This is my very long way of saying...maybe the way you *think* you want something to be isn't, in fact, the best way for it to be. Maybe when you think things aren't going your way, they're going *exactly* your way...you just don't see it yet.

Don't get so caught up in your own plans and way of doing things that you miss out on what could very well be a blessing....on what could actually be a *gift* from God. Look up, friend. Look around. Sometimes a little rain is what you need most.

YEAR 6 | DAY 66

I spent last weekend visiting my mom in Galveston. And though I've been back for days, I keep thinking about the stairs that lead to the beach there and how very much I relate to them.

See, I walked down them several times over the course of the weekend, just taking them as they were, never giving them much thought. That was, until my mom marveled, "I can't believe how much they're covered!"

"Covered?" I asked.

"Oh, yeah, there are a good 10 steps more but now they're covered by sand. This beach has taken a pounding the last few years."

And sure enough, as I looked closer I realized the handrail lowered itself right into the ground. The rails started out fresh and aboveground when they were originally installed, the stairs clear of sand, cracks, and chips. But as time passed and life happened, it was slowly buried.

And I feel like that sometimes. I started out fresh and aboveground, clean, without messy, moving parts. Then life happened. And parts of me were buried by my surroundings and circumstances.

But...just like the stairs...I'm still here. Parts of me may be buried right now...the part that used to run five miles a day...the part that enjoyed spending hours making meals from scratch (I used to say things like, "Why buy salad dressings and pasta sauces when I can make them myself?!" Now I know why.)...the part that had hours of time and endless energy to invest all in myself...those parts are currently about 10 steps under the sand.

My current circumstances don't allow for those things right now. Or maybe they could, but at the expense of things I value more. But they're still there. And when the waves of life finally calm down a bit, when the tide doesn't crash in quite so far up the shore, they'll likely resurface again.

Sometimes when life is hard, you get buried. Sometimes when you're in the trenches, you're just trying to make it out on the other side in one piece. And that's okay....normal, even.

You'll get back to those other parts of you again. Because they're still there and they're still a part of you... even when it doesn't feel like it. Don't lose hope over some sand.

YEAR 6 | DAY 69

My daughter and I started playing a game a few days ago, "this or that." (For the record, she begs to play it and it's *fantastic* for learning more about your kids, especially if you ask them why they chose what they did.)

Me: Cats or dogs?

Her: Dogs!

Me: Polka dots or stripes?

Her: Stripes!

Me: Hey, I'm always asking you the questions! Do you want to try asking *me*?

Her: Hmm, I guess I could try!

Me: Great! What's your question?

Her: (after pausing for deep reflection) ...Poop or bees?

Me: ......what?! They're supposed to be similar...like "ants or bees" maybe!

Her: ...

Me: Bees?! I guess…

Her: Wow, that's surprising…

YEAR 6 | DAY 70

We own a puzzle that was forged in the fires of hell. Just kidding…sort of.

My employer sent me a puzzle as part of a little goodie bag and because I don't "do" puzzles, I immediately handed it over to my six-year-old without giving it a second look. After she had worked on it for an hour or so, she informed me she would be giving up because it was too hard.

Again…*not looking at it at all*…I told her that you can't just give up when something gets hard, that I was *sure* she could do it, that she would feel *so good* once it was completed, and that I would help her get there. Then I looked at the puzzle.

Did you know that puzzles could come in circle shapes? Or that the pieces didn't have to come in the standard square-with-nubs shape? That they can come in tiny little slivers you could lose forever if you sneezed too hard? Did you know some puzzles come with 500 of those stupid shapes?!

Also…did you ever stop to wonder how you would complete a puzzle if a solid third of it was pure black and had no pattern or color clues to help you out? I didn't.

After spending several hours on "the devil's puzzle" as I began calling it, I told my daughter I thought she was right, it *was* too hard. But she parroted me back (possibly mocking me?!), "No, I *know* we can do it, we'll be *so proud* when we finish."

So we kept it...*for 11 days*. Some days we worked on it for hours, others we spent 15 minutes before wandering off to a less frustrating activity. A few times, we cheered triumphantly over finishing a section, only to have my daughter's school rabbit hop through the puzzle to join in our excitement...scattering pieces across the living room. (Pro tip: Don't start puzzles on the floor.)

Sometimes she or I worked on it alone, sometimes together. Twice, we even managed to get others to join in on the "fun"...though to them, it really did seem fun?! And finally...on the last day...Grandpa wouldn't allow us to stop until we finished placing the last 50 or so pieces.

And I was right...I *did* feel proud. (I'm so smart...why doesn't my family listen to me more often?!) I felt victorious and accomplished and relieved. And frankly...I kind of wanted to start another puzzle.

It made me think of our big goals in life. Some days we'll take huge steps towards our dreams. Other days we'll be tired and need a mental break and move just one inch closer. Sometimes if we're lucky, others will come alongside us to push us and sometimes help carry us. (Don't push away their help...never push away help.)

Can I tell you a secret? There's no time limit on your dreams. There's no hard stop that says, "If you don't finish by now, it's too late for you."

Keep at it every day, doing what you can, not beating yourself up over what you can't. And don't give up.

You'll get there. I know you will. And I can't wait to hear all about it.

YEAR 6 | DAY 77

Me: (in a changing room, posing for my daughter's thoughts) So...what do you think?

Daughter: Well, you look like a farmer.

Me: Siiiiigh.

Daughter: But! If that's what *you* like and what makes you happy, *go* for it! It's okay if you don't have a farm...

TRUSTING

YEAR 6 | DAY 80

Yesterday, I set my alarm earlier than usual. I had plans:

8:00 AM: Arrive at the skatepark before it was crowded and sweltering.

9:00 AM: Return home to clean and complete a few errands before I started work at 3:00 pm.

But then…surprisingly…it wasn't crowded. There was literally *one* other kid there when we arrived, plus his dad watching from a picnic table.

And then…it wasn't sweltering at all. Sure, it was still a little muggy. It *is* south Texas, after all. But with a nice cloud covering and a cool breeze, it was actually kind of gorgeous.

As 9:00 approached, I was abooouuut to give my daughter the countdown. But then I realized…why was I hurrying home? To wash dishes? To wipe down countertops? They'd still be there later. To get ready for work? It wouldn't start for hours.

So instead…we stayed. My daughter skateboarded for a while, then switched to her scooter, then invited me to sit with her for a few minutes in the shade. I cheered her on, listened to an audiobook for a bit, then talked about marriage and parenting and Jesus with another mom who brought her daughter to skateboard too.

259

We got hungry – we had only planned to be there an hour – so I ordered Chick-Fil-A to be delivered to the skatepark. Instructions: "Skatepark – mom on bench." We stayed for *three hours* and left when we'd finally had our fill of the morning.

When a good moment finds you, enjoy it if you can. Sit in it.

Sometimes I get so caught up in my schedule and to-do list (I have a lot to do!) that I blow right past these moments. But…what are we rushing off to? Is it vital? Is it vital right *now*?

Time with your family when everyone's enjoying themselves, no one's whining or fighting, and you haven't hit that point where you're just over whatever it is you're doing – those moments are like magical unicorns that only appear when it's a full moon, Mercury is in retrograde, and the unicorn hunter is pure of heart. (Read: Rare!)

So when they show up, *take them*. Take an extra 10 minutes…or 2 hours. Live life. Breathe it in. Eat a chicken breakfast burrito.

And then return to your plans. They'll still be there when you're done.

But this moment? It won't last for long.

Mom, did you like apple juice when you were a kid? Was it invented yet in the old days?

- my 6-year-old

YEAR 6 | DAY 95

A few nights ago, I decided to take my daughter to our first drive-in movie. The ad for the drive-in boasted food trucks and lawn games. And I had dreams of throwing the air mattress and our favorite blankets in the bed of the truck to watch *Sandlot* in comfort and style. What a *perfect* summer memory, right?

But then...a last-minute change meant we couldn't take the truck. Hello, much-less-comfortable camping chairs set up next to my small Volkswagen Jetta!

It's okay, I told my daughter. We would still have lots of fun!

We left the house early to arrive right when they opened, leaving plenty of time to secure a front-row spot and enjoy the food trucks and lawn games at our leisure. Except...then I couldn't figure out how to get *inside* the darn parking lot. We could see it, but couldn't get to it. *How in the world*?! Despite arriving 45 minutes before the movie was to start, it took us 30 minutes of circling and redirecting and circling again to find the entrance.

I'm so sorry Mom is terrible with directions, I told my daughter. But it's okay! There would still be a little time for food trucks and lawn games.

When we finally arrived in our back-row spot, we excitedly hurried over to the concessions stand. *Now* it would be okay! Except...then we noticed the food truck was clearly not in service and the lawn games hadn't been set up that night. Although we had been hoping for a proper meal, we settled for some Gatorade and peanut butter M&Ms.

It's okay, I told my daughter...and myself. We would still have lots of fun. I mostly believed it.

I struggled to set up our chairs and snacks and bags in the dark, had to think extra hard to remember how to change the radio station from my presets, then learned that after owning the same car for ten years, I had no clue how to turn off the headlights and run the car (for the radio) at the same time. When the drive-in worker came by to ask me if I'd mind turning them off, I asked her if she'd mind showing me how.

By all accounts, this night was a disaster. Except...it wasn't.

Even without the air mattress and food trucks and yard games...even though our start was rushed and stressful... even though I felt awkward and dumb at multiple points in our evening...I watched a classic summer movie with my daughter. We shared M&Ms and blankets and smiling head shakes toward one another when Squints kissed Wendy Peffercorn. We marveled at Benny's sweet moves and held hands when the dog looked extra scary.

It *was* okay! It turned out the things that were flustering and frustrating me weren't really the most important things. They would have been nice details, but weren't actually necessary for creating memories with my daughter.

Please don't stress when you're running late...or when things don't go exactly how you imagined...or if there are not, in fact, any food trucks. More important than capturing a picture-perfect moment, is spending quality time with your loved ones...*however* that comes. It'll all be okay.

TRUSTING

YEAR 6 | DAY 97

Her: Mom, would you like a foot massage?

Me: Um…okay?

Her: (starts massaging my arm *with* her feet and toes)

Me: Oh…no, thank you.

YEAR 6 | DAY 123

I was pretty sick the past two weeks. I've recovered and am no longer contagious but am wiiiiiped from all of it.

Finally feeling a bit better yesterday, I realized just how desperate my daughter was to leave our house and racked my brain for "activities" we could do that required very little *actual* activity.

So we set out for Barnes and Noble, a place she had never been, but one I spent countless hours in during my twenties. As we drove to our "secret" destination, I explained, "This was one of my favorite places when I was younger!"

"*Please* don't take me to an old library!" she groaned. She knows me too well.

When we pulled up to the store, she laughed and yelled, "I *knew* you were taking me to books! This is going to be so boring."

And maybe it would be! But I didn't have the energy or strength to go to a park, so here we were...with the promise of buying her a hot chocolate and one book.

She grumbled as we crossed the parking lot in the rain but looked just a tiny bit interested as we walked through the front door. By the time we reached the children's section, with its decorative arch, colorful seasonal displays and rows and rows of her favorite books, her entire face lit up.

We spent nearly an hour there, as she collected books that looked interesting, then parked on a small bench to study their pages, inviting me to sit beside her. She narrowed it down to a *Dog Man* book, asked me to take a picture of the book she wanted to get next, then settled into a cafe table with her hot chocolate and new book, looking like a small, adorable adult.

Maybe your kids won't enjoy the things you did or do enjoy. It's tempting to skip experiences assuming they'll be bored, that there aren't enough other kids or flashy attractions to hold their interest. But...you might be surprised!

There's a *Daniel Tiger* song that carried us through the terrible twos – "You've gotta try new things 'cause they might taste goooood!" And I've modified (and stopped singing it) to say, "You've gotta try new things 'cause they might be fun!" I always tell her that if she doesn't like an activity, we'll know that for the future. Lesson learned. But as far as she knows, every new thing we try could be her new favorite thing!

She says I'm not always right...but she also says Barnes and Noble is her new favorite place and is begging me to go back tomorrow.

Give everything a shot, momma! You just never know what will stick.

CHAPTER 6 | DANCING

YEAR 6 | DAY 129

I decided to start a tradition with my daughter this summer – an annual girls trip. I imagined us staying on a nearby beach...or glamping a few hours away...or exploring a new city...*so many options!*

When I presented the idea to her, she *loved* it and requested:

1. staying at a hotel with a pool
2. watching a movie at a movie theater
3. playing arcade games at the theater
4. visiting Bass Pro Shop and buying a small toy there to keep as a memory of our trip
5. eating shoestring fries
6. eating ice cream
7. wearing beaded necklaces she made especially for the occasion
8. doing it all less than 15 minutes from our house... because she doesn't like long drives

Womp womp wooooomp. What kind of girls trip is up the street, am I right? It wasn't how I had envisioned kicking off this new tradition.

But then I asked myself the purpose of our annual "girls trip." Was it to explore new locations? Relax on a beach? Let's be honest...traveling with a kid is usually more working, less relaxing. It turned out my purpose was to log quality time with my daughter and to create memories together. And we could technically do those things 15 minutes from our house.

So...we did! We drove to a shopping center that had it all – hotel, movie theater, Bass Pro Shop, restaurants with shoestring fries, and an ice cream parlor. Once we arrived there, we spent the entire afternoon, evening, and next morning within the same square mile. We visited stores and restaurants and a movie theater that we'd visited countless times before...nothing new or exciting...and my daughter *loved* it.

And guess what? We saved loads of travel time...*and* money. And have I mentioned how very stress-free it is to pack for a trip just a few miles away?

Our kids don't need expensive vacations in exotic locations. Those trips are fun when you can take them, of *course*! But you might just be surprised...if you asked your child exactly what *they'd* like to do on a weekend trip...the very mundane things that would bring them joy.

We didn't go anywhere exciting, but I committed to giving my daughter my full attention for those 24 hours. I didn't look down at my phone while we ate ice cream together. I played the dumb *Trolls* song she tortures me with because she insisted it was the *perfect* soundtrack for our "trip." We engaged in constant "chit chat" as she likes to call it, and I was surprised at all of the topics she brought up, all of the things that were on her mind and heart, just waiting for someone to listen.

Our kids don't need expensive, elaborate plans. They need us...to show them that we care, that we're interested in what they like to do and what they have to say. They need us to show them that we enjoy spending time with them, whether it's on a yacht in Jamaica or at an arcade down the street. They need us to wear that stringy, beaded necklace that doesn't match our outfit, but fills their heart with pride and excitement to match their momma.

Our kids need us. That's all. Where will *your* next "trip" be?

My favorite part of being a mom is listing every single snack we have in the house to my family so they can tell me no, those don't sound good.

YEAR 6 | DAY 145

This weekend, my daughter and I decided to take a day trip. We tend to explore the city we live in (San Antonio) but recently realized that nearby San Marcos had a lot of fantastic natural attractions. It boasts one of the world's largest aquifer-driven spring lakes (which can be observed on a glass-bottomed boat tour), a theme park with cave tours, gorgeous outdoor spaces, and loads of amazing local eateries.

The problem is that reaching San Marcos requires just over an hour of driving with my carsick-prone, sometimes impatient, child. She committed to the drive before we left the house, knowing the fun day awaiting us would be worth it. But it's the middle that's the hardest, isn't it? It's the time in-between when you're sick and bored and can't understand why it's taking *so* long, that's incredibly difficult to push through.

But rather than tossing out the drive as a necessary evil, we decided to make it a part of the experience. We chatted about all sorts of things, sang along to some of our favorite songs, and insisted to her stuffy, Bear (despite his squeaky-voiced protests voiced by my daughter), that no, he can't get married yet, he's still a cub. We *decided* to find joy in the journey.

What journey are you facing today? Is it a journey to better health? To a successful career? To saving money for a big goal? What if you chose to find joy in that journey?

What if, on your journey to better health, you decided to try different workouts until you found one you *loved*? Kickboxing? Zumba? Rock climbing?!

What if, on your journey to saving money, you decided to make a game of pinching pennies?

You get the idea. Don't waste your journey. Enjoy it. Or if it's difficult to fully enjoy, find an *aspect* of it that you can enjoy!

Because friend, roughly 95% of our lives will be a journey. Those big day trips, reaching our goal weight, finally nailing that promotion or buying a house...they're exhilarating, but short-lived. Soon the day is over and we're back on the road again. So find something to enjoy along the road.

Joy is a choice. Don't limit it to the big things. Sprinkle it like confetti all over each and every day.

YEAR 6 | DAY 146

Her: Did you know you packed rotten grapes in my school snack today?

Me: Did you know that they're blueberries?

Her: ……hmm.

YEAR 6 | DAY 148

My daughter is an artist. That means that at the end of every day, our kitchen table is piled high with drawings, "comic books," and random letters and words drawn in a variety of styles.

Every night, because I don't have the energy to clean them, I shove them all into a dedicated drawer in my dresser to sort through later. And once every month or two, whenever I can no longer close my dresser drawer, I look through each and every one and decide what to keep and what to toss.

And today, I cried. I cried because I found a *million* pictures drawn specifically for me, always accompanied by "Mom" and "I♡U."

And I cried because I found a million pictures drawn *of* me and her together. And we weren't doing *one* exciting thing in even *one* of the pictures.

In her drawings, we were trick or treating, drawing pictures together (more specifically, drawing pictures of *us*, together), and eating ice cream. I'm holding her hand at the skatepark, pulling her around in a cardboard box (something I loathe but she loves), and pushing her on a swing.

Almost all of these activities...are free. It cost me nothing to walk to the neighborhood park with her...or to drag her in that stupid box that breaks my back...or to hold her hand at the public skatepark.

It turns out the currency of memories for her isn't measured in dollars or extravagant adventures. It's measured in time and attention.

Yes, our theme parks and road trips have been loads of fun. But they weren't drawn. Not even once.

So if you're waiting to make memories until this weekend…if you're waiting on that theme park to open or for those hotel reservations…remember that you can make memories right now…literally…right this second.

Put down this book and join in on whatever your child is doing. Draw together. Walk to the park up the street. Grab a scoop of ice cream just because. Free and sweet and lasting memories are right in front of you for the taking. So…take them!

And the Emmy for Outstanding Lead Actress in a Drama Series goes to...My Daughter, in "Hair Brushing"!

YEAR 6 | DAY 149

This is not my story. It's my friend's story. But she recently shared it with me and asked me to share it with you...in the hopes *you* could see what her mother never could.

My friend's mother passed away a few years ago. She was the most giving woman I'd ever met. She gave and gave and gave, almost *always* to her detriment.

She wasn't always so overworked. When my friend and her siblings were young, life (and stress) was more manageable for her mom. But it seemed as time passed, the more her mother did, the less others did.

Soon her dad stopped helping around the house when he could, choosing instead to sit in front of the TV while her mom cleaned up after dinner. Her siblings wouldn't bother to put away toys when they were finished with them, knowing their mom would always proactively swoop up crayons and toys and backpacks to return them to their proper places. She was *such* a great mom, after all.

Her mother's boss could always count on her to pick up any work he couldn't finish...so he stopped planning well or pushing himself to complete it. The school could always count on her to volunteer for any need...so the other parents didn't feel obligated to help. The church knew she wouldn't say no, so she covered gaps with the children's ministry, ushers, front office, and even janitorial staff when needed. And she did it all in the name of loving others as Jesus did, sacrificing like Jesus did.

At her funeral, everyone who had taken advantage of her stood up to call her things like "faithful" and "dependable." My friend was seething in her seat as she heard over and over again that her mother was so "unselfish."

Of course, her mother *was* an unselfish woman. She thought so little of herself and her own self-care that her health deteriorated year after year until she passed away from a stress-induced health condition.

Was that what Jesus intended when He called us to love others? To give more than we can afford to give until it quite literally kills us?

Nope. Definitely not.

Even God Himself sets boundaries. He tells us what He accepts and what He does not. He tells us that actions have consequences...and He allows us to feel the consequences of our actions rather than coddling us in "love." Sometimes love means holding others accountable to do their part, rather than allowing them to do less and less until they don't know how to run their own dishwasher anymore.

What everyone was *truly* complimenting, whether they knew it or not, was that her mom didn't know how to set boundaries. She didn't know how to say no or how to clearly express that she needed to rest, to insist on it. They were complimenting that she picked up the personal responsibilities that were *theirs* to carry...what an unselfish woman! She always said yes, even while it killed her.

Yes, God called us to carry one another's burdens, to love and serve each other. But He also called each person to take responsibility for their own load.

Sure, there will be days and seasons your spouse works long hours and you do the majority of the housework. There will be times your friend is facing a death or divorce or diagnosis and they'll need your help to carry them through. And sometimes you just do things out of love, like making your child a snack when you know they could make it themselves.

But God didn't create *any* human to carry the personal, daily loads of several people on themselves. And frankly, when you take on someone else's personal responsibilities as your own, you're doing them a disservice. My friend's father couldn't find the spatulas after her mother passed away. Her 23-year-old brother didn't know how to schedule a dentist appointment for himself. Her 27-year-old sister had never filed her own taxes. Mom was always "better at it."

Never setting boundaries or insisting others respect your boundaries doesn't make you unselfish...it makes you burned out and exhausted, often resentful, rarely respected. I know this on a first-hand basis.

Boundaries aren't selfish. They're healthy. They're realistic. They're your best bet for ensuring you can *continue* serving others. (You can't pour from an empty cup!)

Please don't mistake healthy boundaries for a lack of love. Don't let people compliment you at your funeral because you did everything for them. Let them compliment and respect and enjoy a healthy relationship with you because you do everything *with* them...and you're both better for it.

YEAR 6 | DAY 159

My daughter is strong. She's creative, determined, gut-busting funny, and uniquely herself.

But do you know what people compliment her on 99% of the time? She's pretty.

Now don't get me wrong, she *is* a beautiful girl. Her hair is naturally highlighted by the sun, her crystal blue eyes are piercing, and her smile lights up a room. But she's *so much more* than a pretty face.

I see this everywhere...adults doting on young girls for being "pretty" and "beautiful." Those are wonderful and kind words. But if they're the majority of things we point out to our girls as positive...as traits worthy of compliments and admiration...they learn that those are their greatest assets. They learn that those things they were born with – their hair, their eyes, the shape of their bodies – and that they have very little control over, should be played to, highlighted, maintained at all costs.

They learn to become teenagers who worry more than they should about their hair, makeup, clothing, weight, and if others still approve of them. They learn to become women who believe they need bigger breasts, smaller waists, and facelifts to stay relevant and worthy of love and attention as they age. Because in their minds, being "pretty" has always been their best trait.

So what if we kept calling our girls pretty (because we also want them to love their bodies), but complimented them *more* so on their character?

284

What if we marveled at their determination to keep trying until they succeed? What if we cheered them on for showing courage in the face of fear? What if we oohed and ahhed at how thoughtful or funny or strong or confidently unique they were? What if we applauded their passionate pursuit of their interests?

Maybe we could help build their character. Maybe we could teach them that their mental and emotional state is 1000% more important than their physical appearance. Maybe we could teach them that they're beautiful inside *and* out. And maybe one day, they'd know without a doubt that they are so much more than a pretty face.

YEAR 6 | DAY 160

Six-year-old (touching my legs that *I just shaved yesterday*): Hmm, your legs are kind of bumpy!

Me: Don't worry about my legs.

Six-year-old (in all sincerity): I'm not worried, I just wonder if maybe you should brush them?

Get a kid, they said. It'll be fun, they said.

I'm trying to convince my daughter that every "Crisp" she knows is actually named "Chris" and she's not having it.

YEAR 6 | DAY 167

Can I be honest? Parenting is hard.

I write about accepting the chaos, the imperfection, the wild imaginations of our children. I tell stories of returning my child's big emotions with patience and understanding. And for the most part, I do those things.

*But...*that doesn't mean I'm not losing my mind on the inside. My child spent four full days late last week living the life of a mountain lion in our home. She was in full character for a good part of each day, growl-jumping onto the furniture and attempting to speak completely in roars at times.

Then she switched gears to being so wrapped up in her play that she wasn't listening at all for several days. I had to repeat the same thing four, five, even more times until she'd finally pause to listen.

By the time I reached today, I was spent. I was short on sleep and desperate for a nap (that I wouldn't get) before my shift started at 3:00 PM.

And of course, as I leaned into my computer to catch up on emails, she turned into a grandma. She hobbled around, got in my face as I attempted to work, and said in an "old" voice, "You shouldn't spend so much time staring at screens! It'll hurt your eyes!" And then she said it again...and again...and again, as I started reading my emails out loud so that I could hear and process them over her racket.

It's exhausting. Exasperating. It can and will drain you of every ounce of energy and patience in your body, then *keep* draining you into a deficit.

Sure, I'll miss it one day. But today? Today I'm just trying to make it to the end of the day.

And so...I used my lunch break to put her to bed a few minutes early and drive directly to the Walmart down the street, where I bought myself a $10 bouquet of flowers that made me happy.

Yesterday, I took the long way home to listen to just 10 more minutes of my audiobook. The day before that, I relaxed in a hot bath after putting her to bed, where I watched half of a movie on my phone with absolutely no one interrupting or watching loud YouTube videos in the background. The day before *that*, I unapologetically blasted all of my favorite songs from high school while picking up around the house, despite my family's groans and protests.

Self care will look different every day. Sometimes it will mean a massage or girls night out, but some days (most days) it will mean taking the long way home to enjoy an audiobook or rock out to your favorite song. But all of those two, five, and ten-minute intentions? They'll add up.

I would encourage you today, if you're crawling through this week too, to make a list of things that make you happy. It could be treating yourself to a fancy coffee, calling a friend to catch up, taking a quiet walk by yourself, buying a cheap bouquet of flowers, anything really. And every single day for the rest of the week, *do one of those things*.

It'll seem small. Of course, my 10 extra minutes of audiobook didn't immediately and magically change my life. But I've found that taking those moments here and there, making a point of checking them off my list every day without fail, really *has* changed my life.

It's refreshed and recharged me. It's given me the breath I need to push forward with the rest of my day.

And it's reminded me that even though I'm a mother and wife and employee and everything else, I'm still a woman who deserves a little something special every single day. And so are you.

YEAR 6 | DAY 173

My daughter woke me up at 5:00 AM this morning to inform me that she couldn't sleep. I mean...what could I do for her? I couldn't give her melatonin at that time, making a glass of warm milk would have just helped to kickstart her day, and I couldn't do the hard work for her of laying patiently with her eyes closed until she fell back asleep. So I agreed to her request to lay in my bed, then listened to her toss and turn and sigh to herself until my alarm went off at 7:00 AM.

I was frustrated, to say the least. But it had me thinking all day...about how my daughter informs me of all of her needs immediately, even when I can't do anything about it. I know the *second* her stomach is upset, her nose is runny, or her bug bite itches.

It reminded me of Matthew 18:1-5, "At about the same time, the disciples came to Jesus asking, 'Who gets the highest rank in God's kingdom?' For an answer Jesus called over a child, whom He stood in the middle of the room, and said, 'I'm telling you, once and for all, that unless you return to square one and start over like children, you're not even going to get a look at the kingdom, let alone get in. Whoever becomes simple and elemental again, like this child, will rank high in God's kingdom.'"

And it made me wonder...why don't I tell my Father the second I have a need? Why don't I bring every single update to Him? Father, I can't sleep. Father, I don't feel well. Father, I'm frustrated. I'm angry. I'm worried. I'm sad.

Why do I carry a burden for so darn long before I finally break down in tears, making prayer my last resort, a desperate plea?

Maybe God can fix it! Or maybe He can help me through it. Or maybe I can just be obedient when He tells me to be more like a child, rather than stubbornly fighting through everything on my own.

You may think your need is small. Or maybe it seems insignificant in comparison to everything else going on in this world. But it's important to God. And it's important to Him that you come to Him with it...at the very first sign of trouble...even if it's a very small sign.

"Are you tired? Worn out? Burned out on religion? Come to me. Get away with me and you'll recover your life. I'll show you how to take a real rest. Walk with me and work with me — watch how I do it. Learn the unforced rhythms of grace. I won't lay anything heavy or ill-fitting on you. Keep company with me and you'll learn to live freely and lightly" (Matthew 11:28-30).

YEAR 6 | DAY 177

We've been enjoying *gorgeous* weather here in south Texas...which meant our "quick" stop at the park last weekend turned into a lazy, much longer stay as we enjoyed the warm sun and cool breeze.

When we finally returned to our car, my daughter spotted an acorn. She loudly announced her discovery, oohed and ahhed over it, and zeroed in on very unsuccessfully "burying it for the winter." I urged her to hurry, reminding her we had lots more things we had to do that day, but she was too engrossed in what she believed was a rare find.

But as I started to load our things into the car, I looked down to find nearly 100 acorns, all identical to her "rare" find just 10 feet away. It made me wonder how often I get stuck focusing on one thing, or one way of doing things, when there are a million other opportunities out there if I'd just look up. And I realized I've spent most of my life that way.

I fixated on one person in my early 20s, constantly attempting to repair and adjust to a broken relationship when there were thousands of other people in the world who would have been a much better fit.

I fixated on one career field fresh out of college. That focus almost cost me the job that opened a million doors to me...in a completely different field I'd never considered before.

293

I've tried to beat down the doors of hundreds of opportunities that weren't right for me, forced friendships that didn't come naturally and never would, and felt less than for failing to meet standards that weren't important to me in the first place.

If you feel like you're beating your head against a wall today, look up! Look around! You might be surprised to learn what God has for you if you could just zoom out from where you are right now.

YEAR 6 | DAY 181

My daughter just asked me to read her the Christmas list I've been "keeping" every time she's said she wanted something for the past seven months. Well, this is awkward...

YEAR 6 | DAY 183

My dad recently dropped off photos, newspaper clippings, and old ribbons of mine that he found in storage. And although I couldn't remember the majority of races and relays listed on the ribbons, I discovered that I was a pretty consistent third or fourth place.

And I kind of always have been! I was never quite first chair trombone, never the #1 seed on our tennis team, and if we're being honest, after I had been practicing hurdles for nearly a year in high school, my dad, who had never jumped a hurdle in his life, easily beat me at an impromptu race that resulted from his friendly heckling.

And you know what? I'm still a pretty solid adult.

Some kids start reading at three, others at seven or eight. Some kids roll out of the womb to paint like Picasso, some kids grow up into adults who *still* can't draw a recognizable animal. (Me!)

Some kids are natural-born athletes, some are just okay. And they all grow into adults where no one has any idea at what age they read or if they were held back a grade or if they won their third grade spelling bee.

It's so easy to worry about our kids. Will he ever learn to read? Will she ever understand math? Will they make friends? Will they make the varsity team?

I think it was a good thing I was never first chair or first seed or first place – it helped to break a perfectionist mindset that was ruining my self-image at the time. Sure, it hurt at times. But it built character and made band and tennis and track about more than winning – it made it about staying active and spending time with my friends and simply *enjoying* the activity itself.

Whatever you're worried about today with your child, I promise you...it'll work out eventually. He or she will grow up to be an adult who probably won't even remember they were always third place until you bring their ribbons to them...in their adult life where no one knows or cares that they didn't win everything when they were 12. Because life is so much bigger than our ribbons.

YEAR 6 | DAY 198

As if bologna wasn't already classy enough, my six-year-old has decided it tastes best on a hamburger bun and has dubbed them "bologna burgers." We are living at the *height* of sophistication, my friends!

Well, I think I'll go work on my balance now...in case someone buys me a two-wheel scooter for Christmas...

- my child, dropping hints like grenades

YEAR 6 | DAY 210

Me (quizzing my six-year-old at the library): What should you do if someone says, *"Come with me right now!"*?

Her: I would say, "No, thank you."

Me: *No*! You should yell *"Mom!"* at the top of your lungs!

Her: Well, *that* would be rude…to yell in the library.

YEAR 6 | DAY 214

My church offers a *fantastic* children's program – kindergartners through fifth graders enjoy worship played from a stage (similar to "big church"), loads of fun games, age-appropriate activities, and more...and it's my daughter's worst nightmare.

See...pre-pandemic, she was five. And five-year-olds enjoyed a small class of *only* five-years-olds. It offered quieter music and a lot fewer kids. But when everyone returned to "normal," she had become a kindergartner and had graduated to "big kids church."

I walked her in personally. I tried getting her started. I tried handing her off to a friend who volunteered in the children's church and was *so, so* welcoming and encouraging as she greeted her. I even adjusted our schedule to try attending the same services as other kids she knew and was friends with.

But nope! Always tears, always clinging. Instead, she would attend church in the "big service" with me each week...and I always felt defeated.

But one day, I decided to look at it differently. I remembered that I was similar as a kid...always lonely in children's church...always feeling pushed through the door and waiting impatiently for the end of the service. It wasn't that I didn't know or love Jesus – it was that I didn't love big gatherings of people – at church or anywhere.

Yes, children's church has *so much* to offer kids – the story of Jesus and faith told on their level, catered to them.

But...doesn't the "adult service" offer worship and a message as well?

Can't my daughter watch me raise my hands in worship and listen carefully to the sermon and learn something there too? Don't my regular conversations with her about Jesus carry weight and importance in her heart? Doesn't my day-to-day life and dealings with her and others teach her so much more about my faith than a 90-minute service ever could?

It's okay if she doesn't like loud services or other activities. I don't either.

It's okay if she prefers to learn by observing quietly. I'm the same.

It's okay if she prefers the adult service for a period in her life. It certainly won't be the end of the world.

Sure, sometimes kids have to do what they don't want to do, go where they don't want to go. But the fact is that children's church will never be the key to her faith in the first place. Ninety minutes a week will never be enough to help her build her life on the solid foundation that is Christ. It's what we do with the other 9,990 minutes of the week that counts most.

The truth is that the most impactful church they'll ever attend...the most meaningful discipleship they'll take part in...is in their day-to-day life with their family. The rest is just frosting. So I'm not going to stress.

DANCING

My daughter bought me a scrapbooking kit for Mother's Day, her idea. She wanted to create a scrapbook about the two of us. That sounded like a huge chore to tackle all at once, so I suggested we make it one page at a time – one page for each thing she and I did together, just the two of us.

So we have! After we visit the zoo, the aquarium, a road trip to visit Grandma, etc., we choose a picture or two to print, then I sit by and chat while my daughter pastes them down and decorates the pages.

It's required little to no work on my part (just printing the pictures) and has created a fun way to reminisce on our adventure a little while longer, plus capture it for good in the pages of a scrapbook. Try it for yourself and tell me it's not a precious memory. I dare you.

Hmm, looks like a little mouse did our grocery shopping...

- my child, judging my cheese consumption while I unload groceries

YEAR 6 | DAY 222

I just felt super proud and happy because my daughter could look in her closet for clean clothes this morning instead of in the dryer…in case you were wondering how often I fold laundry.

I want my daughter to learn to tell time... but I also want to continue saying, "Go back to bed. It's the middle of the night!" at 6:30 am. Sooooo...

DANCING

My six-year-old just yelled "whoooooa!" when she caught sight of herself in the mirror after accessorizing with bracelets, hat, and shades, and this is the kind of confidence I need in my life.

YEAR 6 | DAY 232

Tense conversations tonight!

Her: I noticed last year that Santa put some things from the dollar store in my stocking...

Me: ...hmm. Well, the dollar store *does* have some great things...

Her: ......

Me: ......

Her: You ever wonder if Santa is...you?

Me: ......

Her: Hmm.

YEAR 6 | DAY 255

My daughter visited my mom and stepdad in Galveston last weekend. Twice a year, I drive her halfway there (about a two-hour drive), where they pick her up and take her the rest of the way.

With the way she loves and anticipates and hypes up these trips, you would think my mom was taking her to carnival rides on the pier, the waterpark, and scuba diving. But in fact, they do almost nothing.

They eat at home, play Monopoly Jr. and cornhole, shoot hoops in the driveway, and watch movies she's seen a million times before.

My daughter's biggest goals on her most recent trip were to (1) build sandcastles, (2) get buried in the sand, and (3) eat popcorn. That's it. And she had the *time of her life* doing those things.

Reflecting on it all today, I don't think it's the actual acts of digging in sand or eating popcorn that thrill her (she could do those things any time)…it's the attention she receives. It's being buried *by* Grandpa, eating popcorn *with* Grandma, sitting *with* her grandparents to watch a movie while they make their own silly commentary.

Our kids don't need huge, exciting plans. Of course, those plans are fun! It's exciting to travel to a new place, wear matching mouse ears at Disney World, or scuba dive in Hawaii. But I believe we can create a very close experience simply by giving our kids our undivided attention for a weekend.

We can do mundane things while being fully present with them, no phone in hand, and fill their cups with everyday love and attention. We can listen without interruption, ask questions about them and the things they're interested in, and tell them what we were like when we were kids.

So go! Go do some everyday, regular thing with your kids, but give them your full attention while you do it. You might just be pleasantly surprised at the connection you make.

YEAR 6 | DAY 260

Today, I started a new (temporary) schedule. After working from 3:00 PM to midnight for the last three years, I clocked in to my 7:00 AM to 4:00 PM shift this morning with my ride or die, cold brew coffee.

By 4:00 PM, I was feeling it. And by the time I tucked my daughter into bed at 7:30 PM? Foggedaboutit!

I looked at the stovetop, still covered in grease from the hamburgers I made for lunch…then at the kitchen counters and sink, still piled high with dishes from lunch *and* dinner…then remembered I needed to start a load of laundry if I wanted to wear clean clothes the next day. And defeat settled in. All I wanted to do was go to bed for the night…and I almost did!

But then I figured the grease would only get worse overnight, so I took three minutes to wipe down the stovetop. To wipe *that* down, I had to move the skillet and air fryer basket into the sink…so I figured I might as well take five more minutes to throw the dishes in the dishwasher.

As I went through the motions around the kitchen, it almost didn't seem so bad! Before I knew it, I was wiping down countertops, starting laundry, returning a few misplaced items to their proper places, even filling up the bathrooms with toilet paper! Soon, thirty minutes had flown by and my house felt manageable again.

If you're feeling overwhelmed by something today… defeated, exhausted, somehow completely apathetic but also extra annoyed (Or is that just me?)...maybe you just need to start! Start small. Commit to a small task, to five short minutes, then see where it takes you.

How's the law go? An object at rest stays at rest and an object in motion *stays* in motion.

I used to do this when I was younger. I'd tell myself I didn't have to do a hard workout...I just had to go to the gym and walk for 20 minutes. So I'd slump through the door, step onto a treadmill, and walk at the pace of a snail. But the more I walked, the more energy I had. And as a few more minutes would pass, I would sincerely *want* to do more. I could tell that my *body* wanted to do more.

Don't allow yourself to feel overwhelmed by the task in front of you. Just move. Just start. Inertia (and possibly cold brew) will take it from there.

DANCING

YEAR 6 | DAY 273

Perhaps an unpopular opinion, but I don't force my daughter to tell me she loves me. If I share words of affection, complimenting her character or telling her how thankful I am to be her mom, I don't dictate her response...or even demand that she *have* a response. And if she says she doesn't want a hug or a cuddle, I let her know that's absolutely fine...and make sure my tone, facial expressions, and body language back up that message.

Why? For starters, I want her to know that I respect her as a person. She may only be a child, but she's still a human being.

Also, I don't want her to grow up believing that she *owes* anyone affection. That's a mindset that has done powerful damage to countless people. I don't want her to say things she doesn't mean because she feels obligated to say it, or do things she doesn't want to do strictly because she doesn't want to hurt someone's feelings. And sometimes it *does* hurt my feelings!

But instead of pouting or complaining or telling her she ought to be thankful to have a mom at all, I smile, wink the wink I only give to her, and tell her, "Maybe next time!"

And then, every other time, I hug and hug and hug. When she chooses to snuggle in beside me, I twist and contort my body into the world's comfiest chair and rub her back or play with her hair while she dramatically oohs and ahhs. I tell her how much I love her at *least* ten times a day and also (equally important, I feel) how much I enjoy spending time with her. And when she's not in the mood for that closeness? "Maybe next time!"

It felt like a gamble at first. Was I raising an emotionless child with a heart of stone, who could confidently (and kindly, of course!) say no to physical affection? Would she grow up to never learn how to express her feelings or to receive and process the feelings of others?! Maybe that will happen one day! But today?

Today she knows and kindly exercises her boundaries with family, friends, and strangers...something I couldn't do until I was well into my 30s. Today, when she's upset or afraid or happy or just wants to feel cozy and safe...she runs straight into the arms of her momma. And when she says "I love you, mom" and "I'm thankful you're my mommy" and "you're the best mom in the whole world," I know it's genuine. Because I didn't coerce the words out of her mouth.

You might disagree. That's okay! Your child might have a completely different personality or collection of experiences that require you to take a different approach. And that's okay too! I'm thrilled if you're a parent who knows and understands your child well enough to know that not every opinion on parenting is for you.

But if your child is like mine, I would encourage you to try respecting their boundaries...even when they seem silly...even if you don't understand them. Try doing it without guilting or gaslighting them. Put yourself out there, pile all of the affection you can on them, and let

314

them know without a shadow of a doubt that *you* are a safe place to land.

Sometimes they may not want to land with you. But often, they will. And when they do, it will be that much sweeter for the both of you because you'll both know they had a choice...and they chose to be there.

YEAR 6 | DAY 280

Just overheard a few lines of my six-year-old's impromptu shower song:

"It was as beautiful...as roses in the wiiiiind!
 It was as beautiful...as pork on the griiiiiill!"

YEAR 6 | DAY 289

My favorite part of writing valentines with my first grader is agonizing over which Mario tattoo best suits each of the 40 recipients.

YEAR 6 | DAY 294

My six-year-old recently watched a movie about a young girl who loved indoor rock climbing. So of *course*, there we were less than a week later...trying indoor rock climbing.

My daughter was disappointed to slap on her rental shoes, race to the wall, and realize that she couldn't easily fly up to the top like the girl in the movie. After giving her a speech about the best things requiring effort and watching a few adults struggle on a challenging wall to prove the point, we tried again. But *this* time, I "challenged" her to climb to a rock/hold just a few inches above her head. When she smashed that goal (her feet barely off the mats), she asked for another...and another.

I slowly inched her goal up the wall, one hold at a time, until she could climb two-thirds of the way up the wall unassisted. I cheered, she beamed in pride, and we spent over two hours there building her skills and confidence.

And it made me wonder...why don't we do that for ourselves? It was obvious to me that my six-year-old wouldn't naturally scale a wall the first time she tried it, yet I've expected *myself* to immediately master a new task at work...lose ten pounds in a week...and reach my blog's website traffic goals within a year...all completely unrealistic goals.

I recently discovered a quote that's sat with me ever since, "You yourself, as much as anybody in the entire universe, deserve your love and affection." Friend...what if we showed ourselves the same love and grace that we so freely give to others? What if we celebrated *our* small successes?

What if we sincerely and loudly cheered for ourselves for learning more about something, instead of beating ourselves up because we're not experts yet? What if we high-fived and praised ourselves for taking a 10-minute walk after dinner, rather than cursing our skinny jeans when they're not quiiiiite comfortable yet?

You, yourself, are just as worthy of love and admiration and support as every other person you give it to. So...*celebrate your progress!*

Because you? You're climbing higher every day...even if it's just one step at a time.

YEAR 6 | DAY 298

After fighting horrible allergies yesterday, I asked my daughter if she felt any better this morning. She said, "I feel so good...I'm *breakdancing*!" then dropped to the floor and started spinning.

I hope your morning starts with this level of enthusiasm.

YEAR 6 | DAY 309

When I was young and cool, I would spend $10 splurging on a coffee or cute Target find. Now as a parent, I spend $10 splurging on a *Pete the Cat* album…just living life on the edge.

YEAR 6 | DAY 310

The world is wild right now. I've spent many sleepless nights this week, sick over everything I've seen in the news, worried about the future. Even my daughter has woken up multiple times each night, struggling to fall and stay asleep.

Last night, I found myself praying for those in danger in other countries, for their families, and really, for all of us. And I found myself begging God for relief, for a peace that lasts and makes for restful nights. I was so very tired of carrying so much.

Then I read my Bible. And God led me to verse after verse about Him being on the throne, even when it appears the world's bullies are in charge. He lead me to the story of Hezekiah in 2 Kings 18-19, where it looked humanly hopeless for God's people and their enemies told them as much, but God sheltered them supernaturally. Then I stumbled upon the story of the persistent widow in Luke 18 and my heart was encouraged to continue in persistent prayer, that God *will* meet us there.

And it put this crazy world back into perspective. And today, life just hit differently. Yes, the world was exactly the same as the day before, with all of the same stressors. But God somehow provided me a peaceful shelter from it all.

My daughter and I were able to chat and share some quiet time together as she drew a bit at the kitchen table after dinner. I danced in my car to some of my favorite songs while running a quick errand. And I felt equipped and empowered to say *no* to the stressors that wanted to steal my joy in those moments.

As I tucked my daughter into bed, I played a beautiful song by Jon Foreman ("The House of God, Forever") that sings the twenty-third psalm after we prayed together. She closed her eyes and imagined herself sitting in the countryside while she listened and hasn't left her bed or even budged a *single* time tonight.

It hasn't lessened my concern or prayers for those suffering around the world or here at home one bit. But I've been reminded that God is our hiding place in times of trouble. And I chose to stay in that hiding place for a while. I pray you and your families can, too.

Psalm 46:1-4 - God is our protection and our strength. He always helps in times of trouble. So we will not be afraid even if the earth shakes, or the mountains fall into the sea, even if the oceans roar and foam, or the mountains shake at the raging sea. There is a river that brings joy to the city of God, the holy place where God Most High lives.

YEAR 6 | DAY 311

What I wanted when I told my child, "Let's sneak by like ninjas!": Quiet, tiptoe action

What I got: Ninja sound effects, somersaults into hiding places, slamming backs into walls to avoid detection

Choose your words wisely today, my friends.

DANCING

Me (walking past the back door): Do you need to go out?

Dog: ...

Me (standing at the door): Do you need to go out?

Dog: ...

Me (hand on the door handle): Do you need to go out?

Dog: ...

Me: (settling into the couch with a snack, child in bed, perfectly positioned and sighing in contentment)

Dog: (jumps at the door to go outside)

YEAR 6 | DAY 316

My daughter's beta fish lived 15 months before it finally died this last weekend. We spent nearly an hour at Petco picking the perfect replacement. The new fish was nervous to enter its Squidward house at first, but never left after it went in. Like, *never*...for 36 hours.

After seeing its tail in the *same exact position* inside the house all day today, no movement at *all*, I lamented over how and when to break the news to her, then planned some secret ops. I put her to bed, letting her believe her fish would eat the dinner she "fed" it, waited until I was positive she was asleep, recruited my husband, then lifted the lid and the house so that he could scoop out the dead fish. And the darn thing just swam right out and ate his dinner...perfectly fine.

The moral of the story: You might not want me pet sitting your fish.

YEAR 6 | DAY 321

Me Friday night: My kid is at Grandma's this weekend! I am going to bed and I'm *not setting an alarm*! Who *knows* how late I'll sleep?!......Should I set one for 11? Just so I don't sleep the day away?......*No! I'm doing it!!*

Me Saturday morning: (wakes up at 8:15 AM)

YEAR 6 | DAY 331

I started a 30-day workout challenge a few days ago. No, I'm not following a special diet or drinking shakes or taking expensive supplements. My goal was to simply follow along with one 15-minute workout every day. Seems pretty doable, right?

Except on the third day of my challenge, my daughter walked in halfway through my workout, gasped dramatically that I didn't invite her to join, and then jumped in beside me. She enjoyed her seven minutes and scolded me to never workout without her again. She even insisted that I print her, her *own* challenge calendar, then promptly taped it next to mine and added three Xs to hers to make us even.

The last few days have been special in many ways. We've sweated together, complimented one another countless times, and marked Xs together at the end of each workout on our matching calendars. It's even provided some great opportunities to talk about feeling frustrated when we can't complete a move perfectly, but doing the best we can in that moment.

But it's also made my workouts *way* more challenging. Now I'm not only trying to huff and puff through each move, but also do it while demonstrating and explaining the move to my child, talking her through feelings of frustration and disappointment, and pausing frequently when she yells, "Wait for me! I need to take off my socks!"

I *promise* you I'm not getting as good of a workout as I could if I simply did it alone...called it "me time."

And I suppose I *could* call it "me time" or "self care" and shut my family out to enjoy just 15 minutes focused all on myself. Except...my daughter tells me every day how much fun she has exercising with me. And I know she won't always *want* to work out with me...or do anything with me at all!

So I stick it out. I demonstrate the moves for her. I encourage her even when she's in a bad mood and I'm exhausted. I pause again and again.

Because when my daughter is older, she won't know or remember if my workouts were 100% focused or slightly distracted. And she won't have noticed the difference between my losing two pounds or three.

But she *will* remember that her momma made time and space for her. She'll know that she was and will always be important to me. And that's worth missing out on a few extra reps.

YEAR 6 | DAY 337

We had a very exciting bedtime tonight, where my child dramatically yelled out with a mouth full of toothpaste, pulled the drain stopper, spit into the sink, fished out a tooth, and marveled, "Wow! Much smaller than I thought!!"

Because it wasn't a tooth. It was a grain of rice from dinner and it took me a good minute to convince her of that. Mom for the buzz kill.

DANCING

YEAR 6 | DAY 338

Me: Sighing in accomplishment, admiring the empty sink and clean countertops after dinner

Also me: Turning around to realize I forgot the dishes on the stovetop

I'll take some nuggets with Chick-fil-A sauce!

- my daughter at Wendy's

DANCING

YEAR 6 | DAY 343

My child was disappointed today to learn that the flea market doesn't sell flea medicine *or* pet fleas. Bummer.

YEAR 6 | DAY 349

Her, working on Legos: Oof, this one is really stuck! Let me get my extractor tool!

Me: (leaning in, wondering where she got an "extractor tool")

Her: (producing my tweezers from her pocket)

I recently created a vision board. Have you heard of them? You create a collage of your short-term and long-term goals on a piece of poster board, display it somewhere you'll see it often, then reap alllll the benefits of motivation and renewed focus every time you walk by it.

I did a laughable job photoshopping my children's book, *Girls Can**, into a photo of books on display at Barnes and Noble. See, I am *determined* to publish this book with a traditional publisher and see it sold in stores everywhere.

I've imagined the trip to Barnes and Noble a hundred times – my family and I looking for it on the shelves, squealing when we find it, then enthusiastically taking pictures with it to commemorate the moment. But before this vision board...my daughter had no idea that was my goal.

When she noticed the vision board hanging on the wall and started inspecting the pictures, she called it out specifically to ask about it. And I, somewhat sheepishly, explained my dream.

And you know what? She was immediately on board. No questions asked.

She asked about the other pictures too. She wanted to know what the strong, kick-butt girl represented. (It was gaining strength and energy through regular exercise.) She asked if she would be a grandma before I could buy my acreage in the country. (Kids are so sweet.)

335

Sometimes it's scary to share our dreams with our kids. But I've found it's *so very beneficial* in setting an example for my daughter!

Because I tell her no, the twenty-sixth publisher has not responded to my book proposal yet, but I'm choosing to remain patient and hopeful, this is par for the course. I've told her that I won't get my acreage for years *but* I can bring elements of it, like growing fruits and vegetables in our backyard, into our home now and am working hard to save money toward that goal. And I've invited her to *join* me in working out for just 15 minutes every night.

It's vulnerable, sharing our goals with our kids, especially when we're not convinced ourselves that we'll reach them. But who else will teach them how to dream big, put in the hard work, and then be patient while they wait for those "seeds" to grow? Who will demonstrate not giving up, not losing hope, and trusting the process? And *how rewarding* will it be to celebrate with them when you finally reach that goal and they *know* all of the blood, sweat, and tears you've invested into getting there?

Don't keep your dreams to yourself, friend! The sweetest goals, the most satisfying achievements, are those reached together.

*Edited to add: I've reached my goal since writing this entry! You can find my children's picture book, *Girls Can*, everywhere books are sold. And yes, I squealed and cried and took a million pictures at the bookstore. Your goals are on their way too!

YEAR 6 | DAY 352

Marriage is mostly just bumping the thermostat a few degrees warmer and then acting surprised when your spouse discovers it...over and over again for the rest of your lives.

YEAR 6 | DAY 362

Can I let you in on a little secret? I hosted Easter dinner last weekend…and I didn't cook any of it. My BFF, Cracker Barrel, did. They did all of the heavy lifting in the kitchen and then loaded it into my car, where I could drive it to my refrigerator and pop it in the oven the next day.

It gets worse. We used…gasp!…paper plates. The nice Chinet ones, of course, because I'm not a monster.

Then I paired my fancy disposable plates with the leftover napkins and plastic cutlery from our last get-together. (Somehow the clear plastic forks seem slightly nicer than the white ones?!) I divided them into mason jars for easy access for guests, threw some plastic cups with a Sharpie for names on the counter, and called it a day.

And guess what? *No one cared.*

The fact is, we get together with our family because we love them and want to celebrate the holidays with them, not because we're foodies. I invite them to sit at our table to visit and laugh together, not to admire my place settings or fine china.

It might be different if I really enjoyed spending hours in the kitchen. But…I don't! And if interior design were my passion, I'd probably put more effort into pairing the right colors and textures to give the perfect pastel Easter vibe.

But the truth is, anything I cleaned and arranged perfectly was going to be immediately messed up by young children with sticky fingers and by adults doing normal things – scooping food onto plates, pouring drinks, etc. I would rather spend my time watching my niece demonstrate her dance recital moves than wincing every time someone sloshed something onto the table cloth. And I would rather sit back and listen to my dad and brother engage in friendly trash talk than spend an hour washing dinner plates and serving trays at the sink.

Go easy on yourself, friend. Life isn't about perfection. It's not about seeing how many likes you can get or taking perfectly color-coordinated family photos. It's about family, friends, faith, sharing memories and quality time and laughs together, and just…being. It's about breathing in the moment, taking it all in, and remembering that tomorrow is promised to no one.

And if you can gain more of those things by warming up pre-made meals or tossing paper plates at the end of the day…then go for it! Those who judge you for those actions weren't there for quality time with you in the first place. And those who compliment your genius Cracker Barrel idea and bring their dishes in disposable containers to extend the stress-free vibe? They're your keepers.

YEAR 7 | DAY 1

In compiling these thoughts and stories, editing and attempting to streamline them into a journey that others could follow, I had to ask myself where I landed. What is at the heart of my accepting imperfection, learning to roll with the punches, and keeping a cool head through it all?

And I think it all boils down to trust. I've learned to trust myself...to consider what parenting books and blogs and podcasts say, but to remember that I am the number one expert on *my* daughter.

No one in this world has spent more time with her than I have. No one has listened to more of her words, watched more of her activities, or asked her more questions. I've learned to trust myself as a mother, if only as a mother to my daughter in particular.

I've learned to trust my daughter...trust that she *will* learn everything she needs to learn in her own timing and in her own way...that her unique personality is not something to improve or mold, but something to observe and help to grow...and that she is an innately good person who deserves the benefit of the doubt.

And I've learned to trust God. I've realized that as much as I love and would die for my daughter, He loves her more and *did* die for her. He wants the best for her even more than I do and is there with her at all times, even when I can't be. Surely He can be trusted to care for her when I fall short.

Parenthood is a messy, exhausting, frustrating, beautiful journey. It requires selflessness and patience and humility and a sense of humor and double shots of espresso.

I pray that these words encourage and make you laugh but most of all, that they reassure you that friend, you are *so* far from alone. We've got this.

About the Author

Deb Preston is an author, editor, wife, mother, amateur gardener, and professional cheese lover. Originally from Iowa, she now lives just outside of San Antonio, Texas with her husband, daughter, unnecessarily loud beagle, and part-lion, part-calico kitty.

Deb always wanted to be an author as a child, but fell back on a more stable career when she gained her BS in Health and Exercise Science at Oral Roberts University and her MA in Management and Leadership at Liberty University. However, she always felt called back to writing, as both a career and ministry.

When her daughter was born, she yearned for an opportunity to laugh, cry, connect with, and encourage other moms in the same crazy boat. She launched her blog in 2017 to meet those needs and has been writing about parenthood, faith, and health ever since.

You can find her writing on DebPreston.com and its social media channels (@debprestonblog), on Her View From Home, or in any of her books.

Also by Deb Preston

DEVOTIONALS

Peace in the Valley: 21 Days of Finding Light in the Darkest Hour, 2019
Word-ly Women: A Small Group Study Guide, 2021

CONTRIBUTING AUTHOR

So God Made a Mother: Tender, Proud, Strong, Faithful, Known, Beautiful, Worthy, and Unforgettable - Just Like You, 2023

CHILDREN'S BOOKS

Girls Can, 2023
Bodies Can, 2024